This Might Be
Too Personal

ALSO BY ALYSSA SHELASKY

Apron Anxiety: My Messy Affairs In and Out of the Kitchen

This Might Be
Too Personal

And Other Intimate Stories

Alyssa Shelasky

ST. MARTIN'S GRIFFIN
NEW YORK

First published in the United States by St. Martin's Griffin,
an imprint of St. Martin's Publishing Group

www.stmartins.com

Designed by Michelle McMillian

The Library of Congress Cataloging-in-Publication Data is available upon request.

ISBN 978-1-250-81088-5 (trade paperback)
ISBN 978-1-250-81089-2 (ebook)

Our books may be purchased in bulk for promotional, educational,
or business use. Please contact your local bookseller or the Macmillan Corporate
and Premium Sales Department at 1-800-221-7945, extension 5442,
or by email at MacmillanSpecialMarkets@macmillan.com.

First Edition: 2022

10 9 8 7 6 5 4 3 2 1

For Hazel, my little fig
and River, my sweetheart

Author's Note

These essays are true stories.

Some names and identifying details have been changed to protect the privacy of others. And occasionally, to keep me out of (more) trouble.

The essence of every chapter lives in my heart and reflects how I remember things happening. It is quite likely that others will remember something, somewhere, differently.

Rest assured, though: I've checked with my most trusted friends, family, and colleagues to confirm, clarify, and refine whatever I can. To that end, if someone *must* give me a spanking, it will be because I *want* one.

Contents

This Might Be
Too Personal

one

Are You Okay?

I wasn't sure if I'd make it across the West Side Highway alive.

Everything about my body and mind was unsteady as I stumbled ahead—and the traffic was coming. I had no shoes on. My eyes were blinded by octagons of tears and particles of cobalt-blue mascara. It was somehow too much to carry my crocodile clutch (fuck clutches), my strappy heels, and the heavy, clunky wedding present in the glittery gift bag, especially because my hands would not stop shaking. So I consolidated the bags, chucked the shoes in the street, and dragged myself to the other side.

That's when my left ankle gave out. It does that sometimes. There is nothing more undignified than gracelessness. I fell to my knees on the sidewalk. My long, silky blush slip dress ripped, revealing my scraped and bleeding legs. But I got right back up and kept on going.

If I turned back—which I would *not*—I could still see Chelsea

Piers, and the big fancy wedding I was running away from. It was not my wedding that I was running away from. I had called off *my* wedding—which would have been much more "indie bride" style— the night before. This wedding was for my now-ex-fiancé's friends, where my now-ex-fiancé was the best man. He was, indeed, the best man: the best man I would ever be in a relationship with, even though I still couldn't marry him.

I had broken his heart the night before while sitting on our beige Pottery Barn couch in our beige one-bedroom rental, in a beige high-rise building in the Flatiron District. After five happy-ish years together and one large diamond ring (which I picked out myself and definitely did not hate), I told him it was over for no reason other than not loving him enough. That's all I had, really. I didn't love him enough or desire him enough or need him enough or want him enough to lock into a lifestyle together forever. I only said the love part, though—why make things more complicated than they had to be?

Whatever words I used or didn't, the breakup was brutal. He was young and sweet-natured and untarnished, and had yet to develop the coping skills for life's cruelties and disappointments. (Neither had I, really, but I was built "tough yet tender." It was my brand from birth.) We both cried all night and I was surprised by how hard it was on my heart, given this was what I wanted. I did love him, and I was going to miss him: his sparkling green eyes, the way he would get ridiculously excited to introduce me to a new restaurant that he hoped I'd think was cool, how he playfully called me "My Loony Lys" whenever I'd start to unravel without explanation. "My Loony Lys" would always make me laugh and temporarily defuse things.

It was savage to hurt the nicest person in my life like this. But it was worse prolonging the pain. I wasn't coming home at night. Some of his friends had seen me out at clubs and off the rails. My life was full of moral ambiguity, but I couldn't bear to make a fool out of him.

My new job as a reporter at *Us Weekly* and my new crowd that liked to party kept me fluttering around the city till the sun came up. The nightlife was all heat and sting and it felt like exactly the place I wanted to be, doing exactly the things I wanted to be doing. It was like: double dates and sake bombs with Cornell frat boys turned starter bankers, or drinking and smoking all night long with celebrities, supermodels, and rock stars? *You tell me.*

Every other night, I was either messing around with Thomas, a womanizing photographer with whiskey dick, or Trevor, a feral musician with a trust fund. There was Jax, just out of jail, who took me on an erotic date to a car wash in Queens. And Paul, from upstate, who liked to go downstate. I was twenty-five years old and it was safe and consensual sexual experimentation—which I found profoundly pleasurable. But I was engaged. And the fact that I wanted to be with everyone but my very square fiancé was an issue. Honest conversations about ethical nonmonogamy and open relationships were not yet a thing for most mainstream couples, and if they had been, maybe we could have found an arrangement that was right for both of us. Though, he was a traditional guy and I semiconsciously did not want to be a wife, and those parameters were pretty well fixed and very much competing.

The morning after I ended things, with our faces chafed from tears and our eyes stinging from sleep deprivation, my ethics suddenly kicked in and I didn't think it was appropriate to be a last-minute no-show at this stupid wedding. We had to go together. By the time we arrived, everyone knew we were over. He had told his friends everything the night before so that no one would wonder why we were "being weird."

At the pre-ceremony cocktail hour (a phrase I hope to never use again), everyone was gossiping about the breakup, which didn't really bother me, but it was unpleasant for him. The murmurs and whispers were practically echoing off the harpsichord. When I went to the bathroom, I overheard two girls, who I'm sure were elliptical thin with *epic* memories from Montauk, talking about me. From the stall, I could only see their perfect pedis in ballet slipper pink. One of the girls was detailing how I once discussed pornography with her boyfriend, which she found to be grossly inappropriate, and the other one added that I was "kind of a whore." It was painful to hear, but I told myself I deserved the social punishment.

Everyone made it abundantly clear that I was the persona non grata, and though it was an intense hour of my life that left some nasty scar tissue, I ultimately respected their loyalty to my ex. These were the people who would get him back on his feet with fantasy baseball leagues and "Rosé All Day" and hookups with cute interns from Merrill and assistant buyers at Bloomingdale's, and he needed them. I never belonged there anyway.

I assumed, however, that I *could* get through this "timelessly elegant" wedding with poise. It was miserable and alienating, but . . . that's what passed champagne and deviled eggs were for, right? When I sat for the ceremony, the only people who wanted to sit next to me were relatives with names like Rhonda and Mordi—and even they weren't so sure about me, energetically. "Kind of a whore" clanged in my head, but I tried to shake it off and hold my shoulders back like a lady. But when I saw my ex walk down the aisle so defeated and embarrassed and exhausted, in the classic tuxedo we had purchased for him, hand in hand, with his first-year bonus check from the investment bank, it was impossible to hold back the tears.

The dam burst open. My whimpers turned into weeping and the weeping turned into sobbing, and suddenly I was fighting for air. I felt so overwhelmed by emotions that I was choking on them. My wailing was loud and appalling and I could not stop. As if I hadn't already caused enough unnecessary noise, my unrelenting shrieks were now ruining the whole ceremony. The more I tried to control them, the more the sobbing and choking were amplified. I was crying myself to death and causing a very unfortunate scene. There was no other option but to remove myself entirely. So, mid-vows, I stood up rudely and inharmoniously, ran toward the emergency exit, and busted out of there. Like a nut. Like a drama queen. Like the dangerous person they'd all warned him I was.

Out on the street, gasping for air, I was stunned by what had just happened. Stunned! But I was free. I had hardly floated away like a pretty little petal, but I was free. And that was goodbye. Loony Lys was out.

Why I took this couple's shimmering wedding gift with me, though, I have no clue. I'd rather have a pap smear than a wedding present. In fact, it was somewhere near the All-Clad aisle one week earlier where I'd made the final decision to call everything off. My mom had taken me to Macy's Cellar to register for cookware and dishware and *where the hell* was I? This could not be my life. My mom saw that I was having trouble functioning in the Cellar, sweating profusely, and not enjoying the experience at all. It was an anxiety attack. She reminded me that I could tell her anything, and forced me to "let it out, already!" So, finally, in front of the stainless-steel pressure cookers, I released all the truth bombs. Everything about getting married felt wrong. I didn't give a shit about having a wedding or becoming a wife. I was already counting the affairs I would need to have to make me feel alive in the marriage—and I had recently started several of them.

My mom didn't seem too surprised by any of it, and she certainly didn't try to turn the bus back around. Hers was the only opinion I ever cared about—then and now. We were always the same kind of complex and unruly woman. She chose a traditional lifestyle with my dad that went against her wild-hearted nature because she'd had a hard childhood and valued stability above any of the whimsical stuff. I had an easy and safe childhood, so I craved trouble, and knew I could get away with it because I had unconditional love and a support system. As such, nothing was more romantic to me than a bad decision.

Without judgment, but also without any room for interpretation, my mother told me that I had to end my duplicitous life and my engagement—and fast. It was monstrous to do this to him, and that's not who I was or how she'd raised me. Plus, she's a Virgo, and had months of compulsive planning to undo.

In the countless breakups I would endure following this chapter of my life, this was the only ending where I truly wounded an innocent man. The rest of the breakups would be even uglier and worse—oh yeah, pull up a seat and a deviled egg—but the guys almost always deserved what they got, as did I. This person did not. And that guilt lived inside me for years to come. A lot would go wrong for me, and I would often wonder if it was karma for the way I'd treated him and the damage that I did—not just to this good person but to my own future trajectory.

So, no, I did not cross the West Side Highway into a world of rainbows and unicorns on that tough, transformative day. Not even close. Although something miraculous *did* happen.

I had just enough wherewithal to comprehend that I couldn't take the subway without any shoes on, but I also needed cash for a taxi if I wanted to shelter somewhere. Since I no longer had a homeland of my own, the only place I could go was my parents' apartment in Brooklyn, several miles away. They had recently followed me to New York from Western Massachusetts, where I grew up and where all our family and roots were. And they were just settling into a parlor-floor apartment in Brooklyn Heights, practically days before the real estate market boomed there.

Searching for an ATM, I caught a reflection of myself in a storefront window. What a wreck. Cherry-red lipstick stained my teeth. Turquoise eyeliner and orange bronzer streaked from my cheekbones to my clavicle; my hair was greasy and tangled from the sleepless night before; blood was splattered all over my limping legs. All of the above was saturated in spit, sweat, toxicity, and uncentered energy. I would have given my left tit—already hanging out—for a tissue. Yet all I could do was put one wobbly bare foot in front of the other and walk on. A Citibank had to be somewhere near Twenty-First Street.

That's the block where I accidentally bumped into somebody. Aggressively. We literally crashed into each other. Like, *Boom*.

"Are you okay?" he asked with a kind voice, absorbing the whole situation in front of him.

I barely looked up.

"You okay there?" he repeated, even kinder, now slightly concerned.

I was in such a daze—a trance, really. So without any acknowledgment of this guy, I said nothing and brushed right past him. *Screw it. I'm a New York woman having the worst day ever with a big bag of glittery grotesquerie and I . . . just . . . cannot . . . right now. He'll get over it.* And he did. He kept walking in his direction and I kept dragging in mine.

And then I realized.

That was Ethan Hawke. That was Ethan fucking Hawke!

Everyone knew Ethan Hawke was my number one celebrity crush. I was a *Reality Bites* superfan. If a friend said they'd choose Ben Stiller over Ethan Hawke, I couldn't so much as look at them again. The Free Winona movement was at the core of my being. At my *Us Weekly* interview just a few months earlier, I told them if I could interview anyone, it would be Ethan Hawke, though I couldn't guarantee any semblance of professionalism if I did. Was that a manifestation of sorts? And more important, Universe, how could this be happening right now? It was beyond belief that the only person who cared about me, in the middle of all this crisis, was Ethan fucking Hawke.

I wanted to turn around and admire him so bad, but I was terrified to turn around too. I couldn't look back at Chelsea Piers and what was now my past and all the chaos I had raised and all the innocence I had destroyed. They were probably just stomping on the glass and cheering, "Mazel tov!" at that very millisecond. I couldn't look back. It was too shameful.

But, wait, that was seriously Ethan Hawke.

I had to turn around. *Come on,* I had to. So, I stopped. I wiped my eyes. I put my boob away. I turned my body around . . . and I swear to God, at that exact moment, Ethan stopped and turned around too. And there we were: me, the deranged lunatic, and him, my Dream Guy, as sexy and grungy as I imagined he'd be, staring at each other under the most flickering, soul-warming New York City sun.

Finally the spinning world stood still. My mind stood still. My naked feet were planted firmly into the earth. Ethan's earth. And then, he smiled. A real, honest-to-goodness human smile that seemed to come from the depths of his being. A friendship smile. And I couldn't help but smile, with all my bruises, with all my heart, right back.

It was an extraordinarily glorious moment in my life. Not just because my celebrity crush was right there lifting me up when I needed it most—although, amazing encounters like that are why I believe in a higher power. It was because this was the catalyzing moment in which I knew I was not a dangerous person. I was just different. And I would stay different. And I would embrace different.

Everything was about to change. I was leaving a world where I would only burn things down, and walking toward a life where I'd actually, eventually, convivially escalate lovers and friends and strangers. It was going to be crushing and thrilling and confusing, and perhaps I'd have to sacrifice having lots of babies and any money and the comforts and touchstones that wise women like my mother genuinely believed mattered. Any chance of a nice and normal life was abandoned that afternoon at Chelsea Piers, scattered in the calla lilies, sprinkled on the salade Niçoise, smashed on by Cole Haan loafers during the horah.

Heartbreak would find me all over the world and I would never be anyone's beloved again—not like that. There was no turning back now, and though that put me on a long and lawless path alone, I never doubted for one second my decision to go romantically rogue. But what exactly was awaiting me? It wasn't a fairy tale. But it *was* the opposite of choking.

Before our soul-whispering smiles lingered on too long, Ethan and I turned around and went our separate ways. But I had the answer to his question: *I will be okay. I will be okay. I will be okay.*

two

See Alyssa Date

He was a doctor who liked to *play doctor,* and I was contractually obligated to go out with him.

Let me explain.

A few years after I broke off my first engagement, *Glamour* magazine hired me to write one of the first ever "love blogs" in magazine-land: *See Alyssa Date.* This was back in the day when Anna Wintour, over at *Vogue,* was still processing the word "blog" and wondering why it sounded so vulgar, and I couldn't help but agree.

Word on the street was that dozens of young female journalists wanted the love blog position, so without fully researching what the column actually entailed, I immediately accepted the offer, blinded by the ego of it all. *How cool! They chose me! Glamour* was so glossy and influential; I felt like I had snuck into a whole new league. And it's not like the material was out of my reach or anything. I was a libidinous, tempestuous, and rebellious twenty-nine-year-old writer who had just moved to LA to live my best life. But, in hindsight, I was also overeager enough to say yes to the gig so quickly and erroneously.

The way the column—which I later learned was "interactive"—worked was that I would post a few paragraphs about my love life each day, and then end each mini-saga with a question for the readers to vote on. For example, "Knowing I want kids someday, should I continue dating the Texan with no testicles?" Or, "Can I really trust a man with a kitty named Pussy? PS Please consider the fact that I am allergic to cats." Or, "Do we all agree that Rob the Slob has one too many red flags?" The Internet Gods then tallied the readers' votes, and I was meant to obey whatever the majority instructed me to do, and report back with details. If the readers wanted me to give the dude with the three DUIs another chance, I'd have a peppermint tea in Santa Monica with him. If the readers believed I should be open-minded about the creepy cardiologist, I would give it the old college try. Did I do everything they said? For the most part, I did. Did I enjoy any of it? No, I did not.

The motivation, and marketing, behind *See Alyssa Date* was that if the readers gave me good enough advice, and I followed it all, they could conceivably get me married. *Woo-hoo, a husband! Just what I wasn't sure I wanted.* The announcement in the print magazine essentially read: "Help this woman get married!" Let me repeat: *Help this woman get married.*

It was such a wildly unwoke concept that could never hold up today. Even then, I knew it was complete and utter nonsense, and actually quite dehumanizing, and I felt guilty participating in such an uncool, heteronormative, every-girl-needs-a-prince type of project. It went against my nature, not just as a natural-born feminist but as an independent and self-reliant woman who had zero interest in thousands of random Americans telling me what to do with my life. Plus, *hello*? I had just knocked all the pieces off the board to live my most authentic life, and here I was again presenting as a woman I was not. It all felt so uncomfortable—and I had no one to blame but myself.

I should have spoken up. I could have just quit! But the reality was: I didn't know how to express these things to the higher-ups yet, nor did I realize I had every right to. My bosses were reasonable, but I was still professionally inexperienced, and simply wasn't familiar with the concepts of "agency" or "advocating for myself." On top of that, *See Alyssa Date* was for all intents and purposes a big success. So I wore the tube top if the readers wanted me to, and I French-kissed the firefighter if they said so. Though some of the readers were haters or stalkers, most of them were in fact caring and sweet—so I made the most of it despite the cringe.

Also, it should be noted that I got paid very well to spend an hour a day banging out two or three paragraphs, "putting myself out there," and hitting send. As Pablo Escobar said, "Everyone has a price," and I guess *Glamour* knew mine. In the meantime, the magazine snagged multitudes upon multitudes of new readers, which meant buckets of money for them, and I was, overnight, depending on whom you asked, a famous relationship writer or a goddamn fool.

Other than the fact that I was completely disgraced by myself, and wasn't mature enough to take ownership of my actions, which was signing up to do the thing, there was a much bigger reason why *See Alyssa Date* was never going to work for me. And that is: I was madly in love with someone who despised the dating blog and wanted nothing to do with it, and nothing else mattered but him.

After calling off my engagement and before starting at *Glamour,* I had fallen passionately in love with a drop-dead gorgeous Greek guy who happened to be my . . . dentist. (I know, I know. Just try to imagine a six-foot-two Mediterranean superbabe in scrubs and get over it, because I sure did.) It was love at first sight: a rush of delirium and desire that I had never experienced in my lifetime. From the moment he said, "So, you're here for a routine cleaning?" I was a goner. It was all over. My life, and my smile, were never routine again.

But we were a tragic love story. He was from an old-school family, and the pressure he felt to marry another Greek was nearly impossible for him to overcome. We were together, and consumed by each other, for three years. Most of his family didn't know about me, and the ones who did pretended I did not exist. But I had hope that we could overcome our obstacles, because we were soul mates and I believed in love, and it was as simple as that. (Ha!) I once wrote a letter to his sister, who was my age, and I assumed a little more modern, saying all I wanted to do was make her brother happy, and to please help us navigate the situation. Apparently, she read it, ripped it up, and ripped him a new one for being with me. Over and over, I practiced saying, in Greek, "All I want to do is love your son. . . . Please let me love your son. . . ." for some grand reveal that I knew, deep down, would never happen.

I even hired a Greek shrink who did not take my insurance to help me understand the reality of what may or may not happen for us in the future. The crazy part was, as a Jew, I already understood all the inner conflict and deep-rooted anxiety around the family. Which is not to say I didn't try to convert myself to Greek Orthodox, because I did, but even the nuns wouldn't take me. They didn't want to endorse a good Greek boy marrying a *xéni*, a stranger. Though I couldn't help but internalize all the rejection, again, as a Jew, I did "get it." It hurt me terribly, but I got it.

Despite the Jesus and gyros of it all, we were a magical couple. We were joyful and loving, gentle with each other's hearts and bodies. I thought about kissing him all day long from my various magazine jobs, and when I'd see him at my seventh-floor walk-up apartment on the Upper East Side, before he could even catch his breath from the voyage up the stairs, I'd crawl into his hoodie sweat-shirt, and under his jeans and take him directly to the closest wall or kitchen counter or shabby-chic bed. He loved and lusted for me, too—I was not delusional about that. But he was terrified of losing his family, and it cut me deep being kept a secret for so long, and our forbidden love affair was becoming, as it does, corrosive.

Just before I turned thirty, I was left with no choice but to accept that he was never going to bring me into his world, even though he kept asking for a little more time. Every day, he promised that he was going to tell everyone the truth, but then his parents' basement would flood or a grandparent would fall or it was Greek Easter or somebody's name day. He . . . just . . . *couldn't*. It was never going to happen, and there was nothing I could do about it. So I gathered all my humanly power to turn the page. That's why I moved to LA. To learn to live without him. To put three thousand miles and an in-sane dating blog between us. Maybe after all that, I'd stand a chance of moving forward. *If only it were so easy.*

As *See Alyssa Date* was either worshiped or ridiculed around the world, I remained emotionally dissociated from all of it because I was constantly thinking of him. It was excruciating. Major producers wanted to turn the column into a scripted TV show and after several emails back and forth, I never even showed up for our face-to-face meeting because I was too busy driving in circles around Laurel Canyon listening to "Leather and Lace" and crying my eyes out into the steering wheel. That's how I spent most days.

I was fixated on him, and whether or not I should have stuck it out for longer or pushed harder or learned to make pastitsio from scratch or how to pronounce *galaktoboureko* with more fervor. My career might have been on the path to something interesting, but my heart was smashed to smithereens. And you want to know the truth? I never stopped loving him and it never stopped hurting. This was the relationship that demolished me in a way I never recovered from—and it's kind of perfect, and a little bit devastating, that I started writing about love just when it proved to be so cruel.

It was a hard year to be a grown-up. *See Alyssa Date* was regretful. I was frustrated with myself for writing such a regressive blog, even though it technically "put me on the map." The anger was probably a bit displaced too, considering I was injured so bad from the breakup and mad at—I don't know . . . Religion? Souvlaki? Life? Perhaps I should have asked the readers to vote on this: *Do I hate this blog with every bone in my body or am I just in unbelievable pain?*

To be fair, *See Alyssa Date* was not all bad. It helped me shape and refine the kind of writer I wanted to be, which was a writer who had a capacity to share deeply personal stories as a way of exploring complicated universal truths. Not at *Glamour,* and not like that, but I'd figure out a better, more progressive, more *me* way.

Vulnerability (on paper, at least) didn't scare me. And somehow I had easy access to my emotions, as shattering as they were at the time. Though I can't say it was worth it—my broken heart was never put back together the same way again—my grief for the Greek made me a better, more sympathetic writer and human when it came to understanding life's expansive beauty and pain.

There was an unconscious motive in becoming a relationship writer as well. Somewhere deep within, I thought that maybe if my work and my words could put some air and space in between my heart and the struggle, then maybe my future relationships would hurt a little less. Perhaps, if I wrote about love, then someday, I could make sense of it.

three

This Might Be Too Personal

After my interview with Sarah Jessica Parker, I had one hour to get the abortion.

SJP was my first cover story for a major magazine, and my first cover story *ever*—an exciting and metamorphic milestone for any aspiring journalist. I was thirty years old, and it felt like the perfect time to cross over from dating blogger to formidable writer, and I was ready for it.

I had rebuilt my life into something as glamorous and devious as I dreamed it could be. Heath Ledger, Matt Damon, Angelina Jolie, George Clooney, Giselle . . . I engaged with all of them, both on and off the record. There was no party I couldn't get into, no red carpet I couldn't waltz down, no Olsen twin I couldn't bum a smoke off of, no Derek Jeter I couldn't grind on, and no deadline I didn't crush. My friend Lisette and I even wound up on the cover of the *National Enquirer* pegged as the girls who broke up Nick Lachey and

Jessica Simpson's marriage, complete with a snapshot of me and Nick getting cozy at a club in Miami. It is a rumor I can neither confirm nor deny but . . . *Nick, I love ya, babe.*

Intercut with all that stardust and excitement and celebrity swag, however, there were also VIP rooms and VIP rooms of social climbers, paparazzi, and coke whores. For every Jennifer Aniston and Julia Roberts, there were slews of Lindsay Lohans and Tila Tequilas. My life was radiating with A-list glamour—every night was more unbelievable than the next—but I had no stomach for the darker side of fame. The fast track was fun while it lasted, but the luster for me had worn off fast, and I was searching for a way to escape the Hervé Léger hamster wheel.

Landing an SJP cover story was a triumphant step in my career, and could lead to dream opportunities like writing for *The New York Times,* which was *the dream.* Work goals aside, no one else could write the story but me. I had heard the whole "You're so Carrie Bradshaw!" thing every day since the show aired on HBO, and of course throughout the duration of my famous-slash-infamous dating blog. This was a compliment, no doubt, but it also made me wince a little that I came off as a knockoff of someone else. I mean, I was this exact messy, flirty, writerly human long before Michael Patrick King had a hit TV show. And there were so many bad Carrie Bradshaw clones around then—with the Louboutins and Cosmopolitans and Magnolia cupcakes—and I found that shit so uncool. So I always recoiled a little when I heard it: *You're the real Carrie Bradshaw!* Sometimes I'd even correct people by saying, "You mean, Carrie Bradshaw is the real me." And then I'd regret sounding so cocky.

Sure, I could see it. My real life and her fictional life *were* uncannily alike. I, too, loved style, and in my own individualistic way. I was a broke-ish shopaholic with no cushion or savings. Neither of us were naturally beautiful, but kind of unconventionally sexy. We both had not-small noses, frizzy hair that I sometimes referred to as "freshly fucked," and, fortunately or unfortunately, I had my Mr. Big (big, and Greek). However, my Mr. Big was now in the past, and never coming back, whether I liked it or not.

The only problem with scoring the SJP cover story was the timing.

My life had taken a hard left turn that month. I had just started dating a mysterious architect who lived on the North Fork of Long Island. He wasn't someone I could see myself with long term, but he was an interesting change of scenery, and I was open-minded. North Fork showered me with presents, dinner reservations, and car services—and after all the unbelonging from my previous relationship, I took comfort in him wanting me in such an outward way. After a few weeks together, North Fork also got me pregnant.

To be fully transparent, it was the first and only time I ever had unprotected sex, and it was a very bad mistake. North Fork immediately proposed after I told him about the positive pregnancy test, and I reluctantly said yes and let him put a big, fat cushion cut on my finger, because I was in a state of shock and extremely freaked out, and up was down and down was up, and everything was happening so fast. To compound the dizzying velocity of it, as I spent more time with North Fork in the following weeks, I sensed that something was not right. I became worried he had serious anger issues. After an incident in a car together, where I witnessed a fit of rage like I'd never seen with anyone before, I started feeling not just concerned about him but increasingly scared for myself. It didn't take long before I realized that I could not—and would not—have a child with this man. The pregnancy, and our relationship, had to end. And the SJP interview was set for the day I was scheduled to deal with it all.

It was a lot. And I was capable of managing a lot, but I wasn't sure I was capable of this. As the day neared in, all I could do was repeat to myself again and again, "There is nothing you can't handle. . . . There is nothing you can't handle. . . ." Maybe if I enshrined that into my being, it would be true.

The press tour was pegged to one of the *Sex and the City* movies, and I was warned in advance, multiple times, by my team at the magazine and especially by SJP's team, to stick to the subject. When you interview a huge celebrity, their PR people are fiercely protective. They hover. They glare. They make you feel like the scum of the earth if you pivot in any which way. The intense chaperoning is kind of a joke and totally demeaning to the journalist (in my opinion) and very awkward for a star who possesses any ounce of emotional intelligence.

SJP had more emotional intelligence than she does stilettos or cosmos or cupcakes, so from the minute I walked in the door, she was working overtime to offset the policing of her PR staff. She was as warm and welcoming as the first day of spring. Genuinely thoughtful and whimsical and kind. They say you should never meet your heroes, but I knew that very second, I'd always be grateful that I met her.

I loved her, but I obviously couldn't tell her what I was going through that day—even though I desperately wanted to. For some reason, I was dying for her to know that all I ever wanted was to be a writer and a mother, and I had made so many mistakes and my life had malfunctioned so bad that soon I'd exit our downtown hotel room for an uptown abortion clinic. The words felt lodged in my chest and I wanted to release them with all my being. But, of course, I couldn't and wouldn't go there.

Maybe I could, however, say something on a lighter note. Maybe I could tell her that she and I were kindred spirits, that everyone had said so forever. And yes, I know that Sarah Jessica Parker is not Carrie Bradshaw. And Carrie Bradshaw is not a real person. But perhaps she'd find a small delight in the symbiosis.

My train of thought begged the question: Why did I need SJP to love me, or at least feign acceptance of me, so bad anyway? Who knows. All I can say is that hanging out with celebrities is a shortcut to a strange and insecure life. And in the spirit of generosity, it's probably what makes these celebrity publicists so salty too; they're feeling strange and insecure all the time.

A lot of celebrity reporters share some version of the same recurring dream. The dream entails an actor or actress realizing that you're actually a smart and interesting person, and not just some gross gossipmonger—and then they actively pursue a friendship with you. My recurring dream consisted of getting a manicure next to Maggie Gyllenhaal somewhere on Atlantic Avenue in Brooklyn, near where we both live in real life. We start talking. It's fun and fluid and it is *her* who is fascinated with me and *me* who's kind of like, *Eh?* about it all. She says she wants to set me up with her brother, Jake. And I'm all, *Whatever, sounds cool.* She calls Jake and tells him she met this amaaaazing new chick, and that when our nails dry, we want to meet him for nachos and margaritas. We all get together at a hip Mexican dive bar; Maggie and I are laughing and dishing like the fast friends we are; Jake is lovestruck out of his mind over me. And that's usually when I wake up.

It's such a wacko dream, especially because when anyone asks me who's the biggest asshole I've ever met through work, the answer is easily Jake Gyllenhaal.

In the press room with SJP, I asked the standard—and carefully preapproved—questions. What was your favorite scene to film? Who were you closest with on set? What do you like to eat after a long day at work? (The answer was a pork chop—a detail that, for some reason, I'll never forget.)

Once we wrapped those mini-conversations up, to my surprise, SJP started asking *me* questions. *Where do you live? How long have you been a writer? Do you like your job?* She was one of those celebrities who make every interaction feel intimate and real, partially to come across as intimate and real, but also to signal that we're all equal, we're all human and it's all good. Behind my friendly journalistic facade, I was yearning in the most primal way to start talking about everything at that very moment. It took all my self-restraint to stay so buttoned-up. But I stopped myself. I was not going to risk terminating my career along with my motherhood all at once.

I enjoyed our interview very much, even though we both stayed in our lanes and played our parts. By the end of our allotted half hour together, SJP's publicist was at bay, and I knew my editors would be pleased with the copy. More so, I was proud of my work and how I'd handled myself, especially on such an emotionally loaded day like that.

And just then, just as I was about to stand up and leave on a high note, Sarah Jessica Parker cleared her throat and said, "This might be too personal, but . . . where did you get that dress?"

What? Stop the music. Sarah Jessica Parker liked my dress? Oh, hell no. *No, no, no, no, no.* All bets were off now. There was nothing I couldn't handle except talking about my outfit with SJP. So instead of simply telling her that the peasant dress was from the Barneys Warehouse Sale, and dirt cheap, and likely mis-tagged, I *had* to tell her that I wore the damn baggy frock because . . . I was feeling bloated . . . and . . . well . . . because . . . "Actually, I'm pregnant!"

And I couldn't help but wonder: *What the fuck had I done?*

Without a moment of hesitation, SJP leaped up and hugged me tight. She hugged me so tight that the publicist nearly had a stroke. She hugged me so tight that I didn't know if I could take myself uptown after that. But more than anything, in that hug, in those anxious hours before my abortion, what I will always remember was how the pure goodness of her embrace—not because she was a famous celebrity but because she was a supportive and empathetic woman—gave me the power to trust myself and my choice.

four

Dahlia

My new friend Dahlia had just confessed to a torrid love affair with a happily married Wall Street gazillionaire who insisted she call him a "dirty little slut," and it goes without saying: I was obsessed.

The lover was stored in Dahlia's phone as "NOTHING," which was how he'd programmed himself in there, and what would light up on her screen every time he texted. "Nothing" was obviously a pseudonym, a cover-up, since he was an internationally renowned CEO—the kind who was on the cover of money magazines and hosted epic TED Talks—and also because, as I mentioned, he was sneaking around on his wife. But mostly, to simply be Nothing to at least one person in the world propelled the CEO into an unparalleled state of pure, throbbing bliss.

Like me, Dahlia was new to D.C.; she had recently moved there from London. A few months earlier, we'd randomly and serendipitously met at a Dupont Circle bookstore, and quickly became each other's only friends in town. I was thirty-two and had just moved to the nation's capital—*you guessed it*—for a guy.

Dahlia looked like a beautiful and exotic female feline and I found her very intriguing. We were the same age, both freelance writers, and had started hanging out about once a week because we liked each other and had no other social options. She was private and guarded from the start yet committed to our friendship, and an inherently cool and unique person (which was an impossible find, for me, in D.C.). I also knew that behind those gun-metal gray-blue eyes she had a secret. And that when that secret came out, it was going to be juicy. Worth the wait. I just wasn't sure what it was.

And then finally, at a local Ethiopian restaurant, as we shared a plate of delectable, stew-y, spicy *something,* she told me about Nothing.

"Elaborate!" I implored. "And I mean now!"

"Okay, so it's called feminization and humiliation," Dahlia explained in a low voice, licking her fingers, while looking around the dark little restaurant to make sure no one could hear us. "I'm just learning about it myself, but apparently, because the CEO's ego is stroked all day long, when he's with me, he just wants to be . . . degraded."

"More. Details. Now!" I roared, shoving a second dish, this one of chickpeas with turmeric, into my mouth, eyes locked on Dahlia's. "Do not leave anything out!"

"So, for example, last week, he had some Harvard Business School conference in Boston, and he had to make a big welcoming speech onstage. I waited for him in his hotel room and when he got back, he wanted me to tell him that he got his period, for the first time, all over the place, and that the Harvard staff and all the students and all his shareholders saw the blood gushing through his pants, and that everyone was laughing uncontrollably at him. He wanted to feel completely humiliated. That totally turned him on. And then . . . we . . . actually . . ."

"GO ON!" I begged.

"Bought him pads and tampons from the store in the middle of the night. And he wore them to a big event, with, like, one thousand people in the audience the next day."

"Wait? Tampons?" I was momentarily bewildered.

(And let me just pause here to say how titillating it was having a friend with better material than me.)

"Yeah. Up the butt," she whispered, using her hands to illustrate a visual.

"Right, right!" How dim of me. "And what did he do with the pads?"

"I drenched one in water, put it in his underwear, and he wore it all day to his appointments . . . and . . . maybe also to a guest appearance on *Shark Tank*."

"Wow. Dahlia. That's . . . not . . . *nothing*."

As we continued to lap up our dinner of lentils and legumes, I learned that the CEO also liked to wear Dahlia's dirty Cosabella thongs to corporate retreats. In the privacy of their hotel rooms, he had an affinity for borrowing Dahlia's tight fishnet stockings and smushing his balls right up in there. He also loved it when Dahlia kicked him hard in the dick. And he trained her so that when they kissed, she'd bite his tongue and lips until they bled. Obviously, he also desired for her to defecate in his mouth . . . but her body would not cooperate.

The only thing helpful I could offer to the conversation was: MiraLAX.

Now, I am not mocking Nothing. I would never judge anyone's erotic or play preferences or where they fall on the spectrum of gender or sexuality, and it *is* a spectrum. We're all normal and we're all freaks, and that's great. Furthermore, I truly believe that it's wonderful when someone knows exactly what they want in the bedroom, isn't afraid to express it, and feels no need to apologize for their dark truths or deepest desires. That the CEO loved to be urinated on while being called a dirty little slut and had the language skills to articulate that, is, well, enviable. It's much healthier than wishing your boyfriend would kiss you deeper or go down on you more, and never saying a word about it.

Compared with Dahlia's, my sex life was as vanilla as a church lady bake sale, but as we continued to meet up at various restaurants and bars around Washington, I drank up her CEO stories with thirst and delight. I've always been comfortable with my sexuality, but I am basically a straight, monogamous, cisgender woman. (When I say "monogamous," I mean that, in the past, I preferred cheating the old-fashioned way: secretly and without getting caught.) In fact, I once submitted a love story to *The New York Times,* and the editor accidentally wrote me back, instead of her colleague, citing, "She's kind of a boring hetero, but I guess that's okay." I guess it *is* okay, but it's certainly not kinktastic.

Dahlia's dalliances were my first brush, in person, with fetish life, and it was riveting. I was used to being the girl with good stories (albeit the boring hetero ones), so I luxuriated in sitting back, shutting up, and absorbing her tales. None of them turned me on sexually, per se, but I was definitely turned on intellectually. Dahlia said that she herself was not turned on by kink either, but that she was madly in love with the CEO and would do anything to make him stay and keep him happy. So, the suitcase she'd lug from hotel room to hotel room, stuffed with studded dog bowls and big black dildos . . . and his secret life that she was entirely responsible for facilitating and concealing . . . and the blind acceptance that he had a wife and kids whom he would never, ever leave for her . . . it was all out of devotion.

Devotion, I understood.

Juxtaposed to Dahlia, I was in a much more sustainable relationship, insomuch as my boyfriend was not married, or menstruating, and we lived together in a cute little house in Capitol Hill. Spike was a popular chef in town. He had starred on *Top Chef* and was something of a local celebrity. We met when I finagled an interview with him for *People* magazine because I had a crush on him from the show, and also had an instinct that we would vibe in real life. And we did. We vibed so hard and so fast that within a few months, I moved in with him in Washington (a city I vibed with a whole lot less). Spike was a hip, funny, scruffy sweetheart; he was one of the most easy-to-love human beings I had ever met, a living, breathing hit of dopamine, and as our love grew, I felt like maybe I was back in karma's good graces. Our party of two had a cool little edge. We were stable *and* sexy, cool yet committed. After a year and a half together, Spike even asked me to marry him with the perfect ruby ring on a summer trip to Greece. (Greece! Oy.)

Marriage *still* didn't necessarily interest me—which, I know, is starting to sound a little bit suspicious, considering that, by now, I'd let three men put a ring on it. Of course, I can defend away all three engagements if I had to. The first time, I was too young. The second time, I was pregnant and my thinking brain was compromised, and frankly, the engagement lasted for four days and I personally don't think it counts. And with Spike, well, I hoped to be with him forever. I wanted to have kids with him and grow old with him, and if tying the knot meant spending the rest of our lives together, I was all in. There were no conflicting issues for me there. He was the best, and we had a beautiful life.

But then Spike hired a slick publicist. And Spike launched several more restaurants and appeared on endless morning TV shows. The Obamas, who were in the White House at the time, adored him, especially Michelle and the girls, who eagerly and often ate at his places. Tom Colicchio would come see him too, and the press just loved that. And then Spike went back on *Top Chef* for *All-Stars* or maybe it was *Masters*—all I knew was that he was always filming in another part of the country, or the world, and I was not invited. He was quickly accelerating toward fame, which was exciting for us as a couple, but I missed him, and I wasn't sure he missed me in the same way.

Most days when he was filming somewhere far off or working eighteen-hour shifts, I would learn about Spike's life—a burrito crawl with Bethenny Frankel or a celebrity volleyball match against Gigi Hadid—through Twitter. He checked in with me as often as he could; but most of the time, it felt like we were living on two different planets. His planet had supermodels and superfans sprinkled all over it, and my planet had one strange creature of a friend and, oh yeah, a book deal.

Apron Anxiety was initially pitched by me as a memoir about my romantic life with a chef, with beginner recipes for kitchen virgins like myself. The essence of the "relationchef" book was that when Spike first met me, I couldn't so much as make a cup of tea, but as our relationship grew, so did my confidence at the stove, and that led to a soulful new way to connect to my partner, and the world around me. Aside from the fact that our relationship had in fact stopped growing, and the only thing I was really connected to was the wine shop down the street, getting the book deal was a great force of positivity in my life. After some practice, I'd miraculously become a great home cook with a knack for food writing. My *Apron Anxiety* sample pages had piqued the interest of a terrific literary agent and a prestigious publisher, and suddenly I was an author in the making. At the same time, I was also drinking screwdrivers by nine A.M., obsessing about Spike cheating on me with fellow Bravolebrities, and wondering—here we go again—if I was in the wrong relationship. As always, I could hide behind my work, but to what end?

Dahlia was the best distraction from all of it. As the months went on, the drama following her and Nothing reached a crescendo.

"I have pictures," she said to me one afternoon as we waited in line for a Georgetown Cupcake. I hadn't heard from Spike in days, which had become the new normal, and was happy to partake in some serious frosting therapy.

"Show me," I barked, panning the bakery to make sure there were no little kids around. We were safe. "Girl. Show me!"

She swiped through her phone and held up a photo for me to see. It was the CEO in a cock cage. And then a dog cage. And other cages. And so on.

"I want to print them and hand them to his wife," she purred, red velvets now cupped in both of our hands as we sleuthed back out onto the street like foxy CIA agents. "I know where they live in Manhattan."

We huddled together, scrolling through the incriminating photos while inhaling our sweets. It was like we were in our own episode of *Homeland: The Dirty Little Slut* season.

When I was with Dahlia, D.C. was always less dreadful. But she was different these days. There is a fine line between love and insanity and Dahlia was walking it (sometimes in six-inch dominatrix heels on a scrotum). Her affair with the CEO had gone from steamy to toxic, and though they were still sexually involved, the CEO was pulling away from her. Despite all the kink, it was actually pretty classic: rich, married man has an affair with a young, pretty coquette, until the young, pretty coquette wants more, and then everyone's life gets blown up. Dahlia was unraveling, and who could blame her?

In the CEO's mounting dismissals of her, it was like she'd been "activated." Like there was a bomb inside her just waiting to go off, but when? She no longer accepted her role as a mistress. She wanted her relationship with the CEO to be on the books. She needed his wife to know about the affair and for them to break up so that he could be with her. She needed MSNBC to know about the affair. She needed the president of the United States to know about the affair. Dahlia was descending deep into the madness of forbidden love. I knew this to be madness like I knew that people who don't drink coffee are not to be trusted, that Hugh Jackman is the nicest human being in Hollywood, and that men who *look like* big penises *have* big penises. Which is to say that I had nothing but empathy for her.

"Will you help me?" she asked, wiping her lips with the back of her hand and looking at me with an urgency I'd never seen in her before. "I don't think I can knock on their front door alone."

My endorphin levels soared. This was so much better than being alone in Capitol Hill wondering if my fiancé was feeding his own pot de crème to Padma.

Dahlia and I were going to commit some crimes of passion.

"Of course. I'm in!" I said, nodding aggressively. "Whatever you need from me."

When Spike finally Skyped me a few nights later, I told him that I wouldn't be around the next day. For once, *I* was the one with the exciting itinerary. As we spoke, I sipped some crisp white wine, and searched the background of his cast house for signs of Brandi Glanville or the like. As he was half-paying attention, I further explained that Dahlia and I were driving to New York and knocking on the CEO's front door to present his wife with an envelope of X-rated photos, including one of her husband with a Chanel pump up his ass.

With that, Spike looked at me like I had lost my mind. But at least he looked at me.

Then he forbade me from going on the destructive road trip, and told me he thought I should end my friendship with Dahlia immediately. He said we were going to get ourselves killed. That seemed a little excessive, but I guess it was good to know that if nothing else, he didn't want to find me dead in a ditch.

"Stay away, Lys," he insisted. "I love you too much to let you do this. I'm serious."

"Whatever. You don't love me," I said, a little bit drunk and a little bit bitter—my typical constitution in D.C. By now, we were almost *always* in a state of low-grade misery.

"Stop it with that." He grimaced.

"Sorry, Spike, but I'm going with Dahlia. If you actually cared about me, you'd be here, or I'd be there, so let's not pretend my well-being is a priority," I snapped.

Why didn't I tell him what was really going on inside? That I knew he loved me, but by this point in my life, I didn't really believe in the power of love anymore. Or maybe I *did* believe in the power of love, but I also knew that love was not enough? Why didn't I tell him that without him around I felt purposeless, and Dahlia reminded me that I was still alive? That I was triggered by rejection, and terrified of more romantic disappointment? Maybe I didn't tell him because he had to get back to work. Maybe I didn't tell him because I thought he wouldn't have had the time or attention span for my feelings anyway. But we should have started talking, *really* talking, at that exact moment, before it was too late.

After a good night's sleep, I woke up with a new perspective on the CEO's wife and our impending ambush. Spike was right. The CEO was an extremely well-connected person and we were two young girls fucking with his work, his money, and his marriage. *Why wouldn't he get us whacked by some first-class assassin?* I was not a girl who played it safe, but this was in fact too dangerous. Furthermore, in regard to his wife, how could I emotionally strike down another woman like that? When I looked at our plan from that angle, I knew

I couldn't and wouldn't go through with it. Dahlia and I had scripted a psycho-thriller that I no longer wanted any part in.

So, that morning, I made up some excuse to delay our mission, and then slowly distanced myself from Dahlia altogether. She'd call me often and I'd pick up occasionally, but I was phasing myself out of the friendship. Perhaps I shouldn't have abandoned her like that. I cared about her. But making contact with his wife became all she could think about, and I couldn't walk our friendship back, even though I tried. Instead I blamed my freelance assignments and the fact that I hadn't started writing my book yet, which was very problematic, and eventually that I was leaving Spike and moving back home to Brooklyn because I couldn't take the isolation and alienation of life with a flirtatious celebrity chef anymore.

Through our infrequent future texts, I learned that Dahlia's ploy to destroy slash marry the CEO got ugly. Very ugly. Lawsuits ugly. Leave the country ugly. The last time we spoke, she said when she finally landed on her feet, after a very dark period of healing and rebuilding, she couldn't kiss someone new without biting them until they bled. "Like Dracula," she said.

I know it's not surprising that things did not end well for Dahlia and her Dirty Little Slut—but whatever Dahlia wanted, she did not get, and it only makes me sad. We were two wild-hearted women who took gambles on life and we lost. And as I started over, yet again, I began metabolizing the reality that the girls like us, the girls with the good stories, might never win at this thing called love, that we might be the ones left with Nothing.

five

Book Party

Here's the deal: all I ever wanted was a cool little life.

I wanted to run around New York with weirdos and snobs and assholes and sexpots. I wanted to live in seventh-floor walk-ups and sun-drenched brownstones and studios that shook like small earthquakes every time the R train whizzed by. I wanted men who were adrenaline and drinks that were jewel-toned and clothes that came from Bergdorf Goodman and Beacon's Closet, and sometimes I also wanted to steal those clothes. I wanted depth. I wanted fluff. I wanted to be loyal *and* unfaithful. Mostly, I wanted to live life as an artist—I know that now. And that label might sound eye-roll worthy and pretentious, which is why it took a long time to try her on for size, but that's the life I was pursuing. A cool little life. An artist's life.

One new crown I wore without any reservations was: author.

I wrote *Apron Anxiety,* a memoir about my love affair with Spike, when I was thirty-five years old. It took a full year of extreme focus and solitude, alone in my 300-square-foot apartment in DUMBO, with a ceiling that (literally) fell down every time it rained, barely eating, barely sleeping, barely seeing the daylight, to get it done. I lost weight. I lost hair. I lost friends. It was the greatest professional accomplishment of my life, but it took every ounce of energy and ambition I had to get there.

The book had been somewhat repurposed after leaving D.C. What was pitched as a love story complete with lasagna recipes turned into a memoir about surviving heartbreak vis à vis centering myself in the kitchen. "Write through the pain!" everyone kept encouraging me, which was great advice, but it's not like writing could magically undo the suffering of another crushing breakup— not just with Spike but with the myth of true love. On the contrary.

As I was trying to recover from walking away from Spike and our engagement, which I knew deep in my gut was right but still eviscerated me (yet again), I was writing about all the feelings in real time. In other words, the work led to an intensification of a heart-break that was already pretty intense. The constant living and reliving of our relationship, and the relentless deterioration of it all, was hard on my psyche. What made for some very vulnerable chapters left me with several picked-at and infected wounds. In follow-up interviews, I called the writing process "cathartic," which it was to some extent, but in carefully memorializing every detail of our beginning, middle, and end, I wasn't sure if I could ever move on. It was as if the Spike heartbreak was now baked—no pun intended— into my bones forever.

In the end, *Apron Anxiety* was a sweet little book about "romantic resilience." And I was labeled—whether it was due to self-mythology or the truth, or a little of both—a Romantic Warrior.

I liked being called a Romantic Warrior. And it felt mostly legitimate, too. I had become very capable of weathering the love storm, and rising up from heartbreak all wiser and stronger and "sexier" for it—or at least that's what I cooked up for podcasters and readers around the world and myself. Sure, it was a little hokey, but my reputation as a badass of the brokenhearted made me feel distinctly feministic and maybe even a little inspirational. And let's face it, it was a whole lot easier framing myself as a Romantic Warrior than, ya know, some big fuckin' loser in love.

But if I'm being completely forthright, as I was interviewed more and more about the book and Romantic Warrior sort of became my identity, there was a secret part of me that wondered if I was nothing more than a hypocrite wearing the right red lipstick. To the readers, I might have had this rad relationship style that implied I could easily glide from one woozy fantasy to the next without too much permanent damage, but in the end, didn't I just want a great boyfriend who would stick? It was like all my heartbreaks had a ring light around them. Yet behind the scenes and on the sly, I was increasingly scared, anxious, and regretful.

Love had messed me up. My heart was weary. I was dying to have kids and starting to feel sick about my age creeping up on me. Dating had only caused me manic joy or chronic pain and the sheer thought of either made me want to cry. The worst part was, in the back of my mind, like a splinter in my brain, I was beginning to wonder if Romantic Warrior was just a euphemism for "unlovable woman in deep, deep denial."

None of my relationships had worked out. None. And there had been so many. Not just the major ones: The mensch fiancé. The Greek. North Fork. Spike. The "maybes" were all busts, too: the percussionist who couldn't keep it in his pants; the CFO close-talker with the tragic cheese habit; the surfer who had a minor stroke every time he ejaculated—seriously it was a fascinating medical condition; the advertising exec who burped so incessantly I suggested he see a gastroenterologist; the quirky copywriter who liked to rub my feet a little too much; the "sort of" celibate Mormon; the hipster whose job it was to put massive, inflatable rats in front of nonunion businesses—he literally had a room just for the big-ass rat; the rabbinical student who just wanted to snuggle; the recovering sex addict who didn't seem so recovered; the dog walker who reeked of weed; the hedge-funder oozing of cosmetic injectables; the perfect man . . . with the micropenis (because of course); the Israeli soldier whose penis was so big that no one could possibly have sex with him (the poor thing); the young Republican who, after a morning-after café au lait, said he had "to go poo-poo-ca-ca" and I couldn't so much as look at him again; and the punchable-face who called himself a pizza connoisseur but really just ate like a pig and wasted food like you cannot begin to imagine.

And the latest lover, a grumpy British artist, a big fat slab of a man with whom I had thunderous sexual chemistry, and who liked to muse, while lying in bed naked together, that I—insert your most posh British accent here—had "a handsome fanny." (NOTE: a fanny is British slang for something that is *not* a tuchus.) For months, I would ask random British tourists in DUMBO if a handsome fanny was a compliment or an insult. The consensus was usually, and thankfully, *compliment*.

The Fat British Slab had recently invited me and my handsome fanny to meet him in Paris for the weekend because a gallery flew him out there for some event. He rented us a plush, but minuscule, hotel room in Le Marais. The room was seriously the size of a small shag rug. And let's be clear: we barely left that shag rug. I was so uncontrollably attracted to this big, awful bloke that my body still trembles as I type this. It's such a raunchy expression but: With him, I could not get enough.

When we did leave the room, we ate our way around town, as you do in Paris. But on our second night out, something made us sick. After forty-eight hours in France, we both came down with the world's most horrific food poisoning. I mean, it was like that scene in *Bridesmaids,* but in our little hotel room, with one quasi-toilet hidden behind half a door. Emotionally and digestively, it was a terrible turn of events. We flew home a few days later, dehydrated and humiliated, and could never look at each other again.

That trip was a metaphor for so many of my relationships. Passion. Nausea. Over.

Did I actually regret dating any of those guys? Not at the time. I mostly loved finding the humanity in these sexy pieces of shit— and that was the problem. Through the years, I'd turned to difficult men like plants to the sun. They were all acquired tastes, who *tasted* like trouble plus a Tic Tac. That's what I liked, and who I liked, and nothing was going to change it. I wasn't going to get struck by lightning and suddenly start dating all the lovely, sensible men with health insurance and Keurig coffee machines and cedar-shingle weekend homes in Sag Harbor, with mattresses that were not on the floor. Those guys did zero for me. They could all lock themselves up and lose the key at the Shinnecock Hills Golf Club for all I cared.

Straight lines scared me. And yet, the abstract was getting old. My stories were getting old. *I* was getting old. Domestic life seemed like death, and yet I was tired of being so untethered. Something had to give. And if there was a single moment that I knew that to be true, it was at my book party.

Now. Do not get me wrong. My book party was one of the happiest nights of my life. It was a killer soiree at a massive industrial bookstore under the Brooklyn Bridge, with spotlights and spritzes and trendy skewers and status chocolate and a breathtaking amount of love and support. And . . . I had earned it! I wrote a book! I wrote a freakin' book! Pure, fizzy joy ran through my bloodstream as I periodically stepped back to take it all in, and to thank God for reminding me, yet again, that when you're open to it, life is a series of sacred moments.

I mean, how many times in one's life do you actually get to witness your own dream come true? For most people, the answer is never. And there I was standing in front of a sea of close friends and rosy strangers, slinking around in a vintage Gucci gown, watching my dreams unfold right in front of my eyes. Surreal. And to add to the magic, my family was there and they looked ravishing. Everything could keep crumbling down with the boyfriends and I would always be okay because of them. The evening was as much about my mom, my dad, and my sister as it was about me, and all our Shelasky feathers were fluffed to the sky that night.

At my party, there was no denying that I had created my cool little life. I saw old and new girlfriends, all of whom I considered to be goddesses, and colleagues and contemporaries who were, to me, New York icons. I saw writers and lovers and haters and readers. And I saw myself as . . . as a not entirely unsuccessful writer. And as—yeah, fuck it—an artist.

But I could not ignore the things I didn't see, either. I could not ignore the blazing absences in my life. I did not see a partner who loved me for exactly who I was, who would hold my hand at my once-in-a-lifetime book party and share that memory with me. I did not see any children cheering for their mama, twirling around in Mini Boden prints and sneaking cake pops and maraschino cherries from the bar. The only absolute truth I knew was that I wanted both of those things, and I did not see a clear path to either as I looked at my universe as a whole.

While my lifestyle, work, and community had amounted to everything I had dreamed of, I knew I could not get stuck there. The baggage of my dating life was building up. What was now a confident, if weatherworn, sense of love and sex, would soon turn to indifference, then bitterness, then remorse, and then it would be over. Something had to change—but what? I wasn't quite sure. The only answer I could come up with was that if change wasn't moving toward me, I had to move toward change.

It was time to slip out the side door, not just from my book party but from myself. There was so much I wanted to say that night, but I was emotionally overwhelmed and kept getting too choked up to deliver any coherent string of words. I wish I had taken that microphone and told my parents that, because they made me feel so loved and safe, I had the privilege—and it was a privilege—to be so wild and free. I wish I told my sister that because she was always behind me paddling, I could ride any waters without feeling afraid. But mostly, I wish I had said: Goodbye. Goodbye, Romantic Warrior. Goodbye, Handsome Fanny. Goodbye, crazy, beautiful New York.

Instead all I could do was put my hand to my heart and whisper the words, "Thank you."

And that was it.

The party was over.

six

May You Be Happy

There was a naughty mom, a Beverly Hills diva, a seventy-five-year-old socialite, and me, and we were all late for the Fondue Tram.

We were in Switzerland—where you're not allowed to be late for anything, especially that which includes gooey cheese melted on crusty bread on a stick—for a press trip, an all-expenses-paid and no-expenses-spared "mini-vacation" for select journalists. The way it works is: A publicist invites you on a press trip to, say, Dijon, France, to learn about mustard, or Newport, Rhode Island, to rock out at the Newport Folk Festival. Everything is "comped"—flight, hotel, meals, drinks, spa, etc. All you have to do is guarantee that you'll write about whoever's footing the bill, which is either the city, the region, or maybe a high-end hotel with a big marketing budget.

Ethically, press trips aren't great. Some people argue that a writer is essentially being bribed into writing about whatever the publicist tells them to write about—even if it's garbage. It's basically a quid-pro-quo arrangement—and in theory, that takes away from the integrity of the reporting and can lead to disingenuous travel articles. Also, all the wonderful small businesses that can't afford a high-end PR company are overshadowed by the big businesses that can. But I tended to look at press trips simply as a way to discover new places, people, and things around the world that I otherwise couldn't afford to do as a scrappy freelancer with a slight TheRealReal problem.

That being said, there's no free lunch. If an article does not come out (which happens all the time; editors can pull the plug on anything they want to for no good reason) or more likely, you never get around to writing the damn thing because you're too busy chasing the next cashmere bathrobe and pink marble hammam—then you find yourself in big trouble. The PR team will hunt you down until you finally write some depthless story, for some hack of a publication, just so they can show the client that you were worth your weight in filet mignon and oxygen facials.

Again, it's not great. But it is free travel, so you suck it up and get it done in the most ethical way you can and c'est la vie.

Traveling through Europe as a travel writer was meant to serve two purposes. The first: self-repair. It was time to rest and digest after publishing *Apron Anxiety*. The book took a toll on me. I felt like I had literally written my heart out. And the second: I hoped that moving through Europe would be a transitional journey into the next chapter in my life. A transition into what? I wasn't sure yet. All I knew was that I was searching for answers on how to find love and have kids while still being me. And if I could conduct that search while sunbathing on the edge of a beach cliff in Croatia? Sign me up.

Which brings me back to the Fondue Tram. Being in Switzerland, I was on a highly organized and structured press trip with a tight schedule, implemented under the close, watchful eye of a Swiss tour guide named Thérèse. Thérèse was not particularly, shall we say, chill. A good way to describe her might be "pleasantly hostile." And yet, she wore mala beads and mentioned her meditation practice more than once. I couldn't put my finger on her. All I knew was that she was a Swiss Buddhist enigma, and she hated us.

Per Thérèse, we journalists were expected to be punctual and professional, and rightly so! We were guests in this lovely country. The only problem was that we four girls—the naughty mom, the diva, the socialite, and me—wanted to be bad. We had incredible alchemy from the moment we met at the Zurich airport, which no one could have expected as writers on press trips often can't stand each other. Not us. We instantly went from complete strangers to soul sisters. Our collective spark was so alive that we were nothing short of high, out of our minds, on life together.

"It's a goddamn press trip, not a female penitentiary," the naughty mom snorted as we made our first loop around a particularly regal area of Zurich, wet Raclette dripping down her pumped-up lips. Read: hero.

They all were my heroes. *She* was already plotting some hotel room tryst with the piano player from the lobby. The diva, who refused to walk *anywhere,* not even a few feet, was on an obsessive-compulsive quest for a white mink muff. The seventy-five-year-old socialite was as majestic as Elizabeth Taylor, though she kept getting runs in her "hose"—and every time she'd say "hose," the four of us, herself included, would spit out our Birchermüesli dying laughing.

The ladies and I toured the entire city having epic laughing attacks, guffawing over absolutely everything and nothing, and it was pure travel magic. At one point, I had such bad carsickness (a lifelong thing) that I was cackling AND puking from the floor of our van, and I genuinely believed I'd gone insane.

Part two of the trip included a few nights at the iconic Gstaad Palace, where a Coca-Cola is forty-two dollars and European royals would sit next to us at lunch. By now Thérèse thought we were all monsters and wanted to strangle us with her mala beads, so to up the ante, I set up online dating accounts for us four girls to toy with on our off hours. We were all single, besides the naughty mom, who was about to get divorced, and starved for hot sex.

None of our Swiss lovers panned out, but they all made for great material. Mine was a boy named Pere, as in the produce called "pear," and though we had no chemistry whatsoever, the girls and I sure had fun with his name over our fruit bowls the next morning. Oh, we were awful. We crashed a private Duran Duran concert in our pajamas, and the police came. We told a bunch of handsome oil tycoons—who were not even looking in our direction—that we would never, ever fuck them because they were ruining our planet. Everything we did was rude and inappropriate, and though we were all classy ladies back in the real world, in Switzerland we just could not help ourselves. Thérèse, clutching her positive energy trinkets, regretted the day we were given passports.

I booked myself on almost ten press trips that year, most of which I behaved adequately on. In Sri Lanka, I hiked through the rain forest *and* the jungle, then illegally downloaded the *Breaking Bad* finale and watched it with monkeys in my hut. In Amsterdam, I ate one too many watermelon-flavored edibles and wound up hiding under my bed, debating with myself whether Jon Hamm was cool or a douche. (Inconclusive.) In Dubrovnik, I hunkered down at a secret beach club on the Adriatic Sea, while sipping a cold beer and tearing through *Gone Girl*. Next, I was off to Italy, and then it was time to go home. Was I a new woman? Not really. But there were small personal evolutions happening everywhere and I knew they were only for the better.

On our last night in Switzerland, Thérèse instructed us to dress warm, wear our snow boots, and meet outside the hotel at eight P.M. for a little surprise. It was dark out and freezing, but the diva had triumphantly purchased her white fur outerwear and the rest of us were all layered up. As we followed Thérèse into the woods (with the diva on my back, all ninety pounds of her, not including the mink), we had no idea where we were going. In transit, the naughty mom handed each of us our own little flasks filled with brandy. She even gave one to Thérèse, who did not have to think twice about drinking.

After a ten-minute trek through the woods, with our heart rates up and our boots crunching through the snow, there was a large opening in the trees. An elegant horse-drawn carriage stood there awaiting us. It was like we had walked into a dream. Thérèse said we were heading through a mystic forest to ultimately land at a small log cabin in the countryside, where a rustic home-cooked meal would be served to us in front of a fireplace. We cheered and jumped for joy! One by one, we hopped into the back of the royal carriage. We were so excited that Thérèse had planned something so special for us that once we were all nestled in, we each found a way to hug and kiss her, whether she liked it or not. Turns out, she quite liked it. She was relieved that we loved the surprise so much. Then the five of us went dashing through the snow, laughing all the way.

The air was cold and crisp, and we were surrounded by beautiful mountains lit only by the moon. As our flasks warmed our bodies, we recapped the trip, all giddy and tipsy and close. But we were also a little quiet, for us. We wanted to take in the entrancing sounds of nature at night, set to the dramatic gallops of our horse. Maybe it was the affiliated benefits of Thérèse's relationship to Buddha, but we wanted to be as present as possible. And in our giddy-tipsy-present journey from the Gstaad Hotel into the calm of the earth, I noticed that I was . . . purely happy. There, somewhere in another world, far away from the worries of my future and the residue of my past, I felt like a little girl again. And it was glorious.

After we dismounted the carriage, Thérèse asked us all to stand on our own two feet, take a deep breath, and be still. We were surrounded only by the trees, snow, stars, moon, mountain air, and womanly energy. She asked us to close our eyes.

"Is this where she murders us?" the socialite whispered. "Because I kinda thought she liked us now?"

Confounded, I looked at her and shrugged.

"I said close your eyes, you crazy bitches," Thérèse commanded again, and this time, I knew indeed she liked us.

For the first time since landing in Switzerland, we did what we were told. We closed our eyes. We centered our bodies. We breathed.

"Repeat after me: May I be happy."

May I be happy.

"May I be healthy."

May I be healthy.

"May I be safe."

May I be safe.

"May I live with ease."

May I live with ease.

seven

A Foreign Tongue

I was running through the streets of Rome with a bushy-haired man who was searching for Jesus Christ's "stolen foreskin" when I realized: this was exactly where I was meant to be.

It all started on a press trip to Pantelleria, a mystifying Italian holiday spot between Sicily and Tunisia, where chic Europeans would go to lose themselves in caperberries, lava cliffs, and untouched beauty. It wasn't my favorite place on earth, but it was certainly a poetic hideaway where I could reflect on my travels thus far.

The most important thing to know about Pantelleria, in this case, was that it led me to Rome. On the way back to the States, we had a six-hour layover there. And within the confines of those six hours, I met up with an Italophile writer friend, David Farley—who had written a book about the hunt for Christ's foreskin, which is apparently a thing, and which unbeknownst to most people, is a thing that had gone missing. Farley swooped me up at the airport and said we had just enough time for a plate of cacio e pepe in the city.

It was dusk in Italy. I had never been to Rome or heard of cacio e pepe before, and I wasn't particularly interested in any relics having to do with Jesus's old junk, but thanks to Farley's sense of adventure, I was immediately lovestruck by the city. Rome was badly behaved and spiritually intense. Rome was hip, yet resistant to change. Rome was glamorous and confrontational and oversensitive and tough. Rome felt a lot like . . . me. And it was there that I knew I could keep figuring out my future in a groovy and doable way. As Farley and I rushed back to the airport so I could make my flight, I swore I'd return soon.

One month later I rented an Airbnb that was promised to be a "chic, airy loft in Monti." Farley and I had touched on the edge of the neighborhood while finding the right place to eat, and I made a mental note that I liked it there. My stay was meant to be for three months, giving me just enough time to start writing a new book, which I briefly considered calling *How to F*ck Him and Feed Him*. (It was going to include recipes, and *other* tips.) To the eye, Monti was all cobblestone streets and small fashion boutiques. To the ear, it was clanging plates from local trattorias and artsy Italians passionately swearing at each other. It seemed like the perfect starting point to live, listen, think, and write.

But I didn't really know the area at all. I didn't know if it was near the Pope or the Colosseum. All I knew was which train to take from the airport and from there, I would have to ask for directions. That said, nothing feels worse than acting like a tourist. So as I found myself completely disoriented outside of Rome's main train station, huffing and puffing against my overstuffed black suitcase, wearing an Urban Outfitters hoodie that read *Text Me When You Get Home* with handfuls of Haribo candy jammed in my cheeks, I was rather mortified to be me.

Over by a beautiful old fountain—which basically places you anywhere in Rome—I saw someone who looked like a dependable local. He was a big, commanding guy. Ugly-sexy. Slumped over a dusty silver Vespa. Hand-rolling a cigarette. Could I have asked a helpful little nun to draw me a quick, easy map? Sure. But have you met me? I floated straight to Ugly-Sexy.

"*Scusi, parla inglese?* Do you know where 25 Via della Madonna dei Monti is?"

"Yeah . . ."

"Oh, so you speak English!"

"Yeah . . ."

"So, can you tell me how to get there?"

He whistled through his fingers for a taxi, and then told the driver in Italian to take my bags to 25 Via della Madonna dei Monti.

With my luggage now ostensibly *gone,* he looked me straight in the face and said, "Hop on, *bella.*"

I hopped on. And I stayed on. For a motherfucking year.

His name was Daniel. And he called me "Bella." He was a Roman Jew, which—not yet knowing there are quite a few Roman Jews—I found unbelievably fateful. Part of me actually thought God had sent him my way. A divine intervention in the form of a big jerk with a Jewish heart and, hopefully, a high sperm count. Yes, Daniel was not exactly a lovebug. He came off as arrogant, critical, and particular. But he was an interesting man who made me feel curious and sensuous.

He owned a little business in Monti. I couldn't tell if everyone in the neighborhood respected him or despised him, and frankly, I wasn't sure where I stood on the matter either. But I *was* drawn to him, and superficially, I loved the optics of it all. Zooming around Rome on a Vespa, with a sexy beast who kissed with so much tongue that it felt like choke-play, all the way to Shabbos dinner? Are you kidding me? Dreams do come true.

Because of Daniel, I decided to stay in Rome longer than the three months. I pulled every string and favor I could for a job as *Condé Nast Traveler*'s online Rome correspondent, a coveted gig that had just opened up at the exact right time. To my extreme delight, I landed the job. The next day, I bought a pesto-green vintage bike from an old man named Giacomo at a flea market. Then I named the bike Giacomo and rode him everywhere for work and play: to interviews with pizzaiolos and architects and expats; to long, cinematic bike rides around Villa Borghese; to the biggest Zara in the country somewhere near Palazzo Bocconi. Giacomo the Bike took me to ancient churches where I meditated, and to food markets where I'd find myself flirting with artichokes and cherries. Did I feel present, happy, and whole? More than not, I certainly did. The espressos were better than drugs; the pasta was better than sex. Who wouldn't feel present, happy, and whole? Life was looking good.

Daniel thought I was a cute, fun, free-spirited American. *A beach read*. To ensure that he knew I was a lot more than that, early on, I told him that I was on a worldwide mission to figure out how to find love and have children without deviating from myself. He didn't seem too threatened by that, which I took as a good sign, allowing me to take our relationship a lot more seriously. We had heat, and religion, and an intoxicating lifestyle, and I liked being with him a lot. Mr. Personality, he was not. He was an asshole-touched-by-magic, my favorite breed of men. But I still had hope that life with him could be sustainable. He wasn't the safest bet, but I could see us working out. I had become obsessed with the idea of living between Brooklyn and Rome. My parents were already on board, mapping out summers in Tuscany and grandkids named Francesca and Alessandro. My sister and I sketched out a business plan for a jet-set-y tote bag collection that came with well-cultured travel itineraries called "Emotional Baggage." She bought the URL and everything.

Then, after six months in Italy, I lost my job with *Condé Nast Traveler*. They said they were "restructuring," but the editor and I never found our groove, and I think she found someone more competent, maybe someone who actually spoke Italian. I had never lost a job before and felt like the rug had been pulled out from under me, but at least I had more time to cultivate my nonexistent next book deal and my life with Daniel. It also freed me up to crank out a few stories about Italy for various magazines, including one piece for *New York* magazine that was inspired by my loudmouth neighbors in Monti. It was titled "12 Ways to Say 'Screw You' in Italian." My favorite phrases on the list were, *Prendila in culo da un ciuccio imbizzarrito.* Translation: "Take it in your ass from a runaway donkey." And, *Ti metto un remo in culo e ti sventolo per l'aria,* which means, "I will stick an oar in your ass and wave you like a flag."

As my relationship with Daniel strengthened, we started talking about getting pregnant in a real way. He wasn't sure he was ready quite yet, but he thought he might be soon. His answer placated me for the time being, even if we had different interpretations of the meaning of "soon." For the next few months, we cooked together every night, we hosted dinner parties, we blew lines at a club, we celebrated my thirty-seventh birthday on a gondola in Venice, we ate shakshuka in the shade in Tel Aviv, and we skinny-dipped in Saint-Tropez.

After a year together, I asked about getting pregnant again. This time, the more I pushed (I was that much closer to forty), the more he pulled away. And the more he pulled away, the more my pregnancy longings, or "flare-ups," as I'd come to think of them, became urgent and despairing. We started fighting all the time. When he continued to respond astringently and unfavorably to my pregnancy pleas—now snarling that he was very much not ready and did not appreciate being backed into a corner, and that I was acting hysterical and it was not sexy at all—I would completely lose touch with all the balance and joy that I had collected throughout my time abroad; it was like it all got erased. Try being zen when you're absolutely dying to get pregnant and getting older by the millisecond. Trust me, it's tough. When I tried to calm down, I couldn't even remember the magical words we said in the mountains of Switzerland.

One day we decided to take a break from ourselves and have lunch near the top of the Spanish Steps. It was a beautiful spring day in Roma, and I was feeling optimistic about life despite all our volatility.

"It's such a gorgeous afternoon"—I smiled—"and we've been doing so well. . . . When was the last time we even had a really big fight? All relationships ebb and flow, ya know? This too shall—"

"Bella," he said, interrupting me fiercely, his eyes so red, they looked like blood oranges.

"What?" I asked, my heart sinking, desperate not to hear the next words out of his mouth.

"Bella." He frowned. "I don't think I want to have children. And I don't think I want to be in a relationship. I think I'm supposed to be alone. I think I am *destined* to be alone."

"No, Daniel. Don't say that," I begged. "No one wants to be alone. You don't mean that! Please tell me you don't mean that. . . ."

He meant it. And there was nothing I could say or do to change his mind. When someone has fallen out of love with you, they never come back.

And while I deeply despise that trope of a woman *pushing* a man to get her pregnant and the man "running for the hills," that is literally what happened here. I pushed Daniel to get me pregnant. And he ran for the hills. The Himalayas, to be specific.

"I'm leaving tomorrow," he said, now weeping himself. "I'm going to live in a yurt, in India. By myself. For a very long time. I am so sorry."

I was devastated. Daniel's rejection of me, and our Brooklyn-Roman babies, my Francesca and Alessandro, destroyed me. He was hardly the greatest love of my life, but our breakup was a life quake I did not see coming. Or, worse, it was a life quake I *did* see coming and had somehow set myself up for, because I could not *do* *love* any other way. Regardless. It was another horrible breakup. Another romantic misstep. Another embarrassment in front of my family, friends, and readers who were rooting for me against all odds. Another slap in the face from the universe that I kept on trusting despite my pitiful reality.

Later that night, we said our goodbyes. Over strong negronis in a dark, noisy bar, I looked at him and wept oceans of tears. The disappointment I felt was overwhelming. Not just in Daniel but in life. I was thirty-seven. I wanted kids. Everybody will not get everything, but I *needed* to have kids. What the hell was I going to do? All my relationships were good for nothing but a few personal essays on love and loss for six hundred dollars a pop. So, how could I not cry? My life had not worked out. *My life had not worked out.* How could I not cry forever?

"I never knew that you were so pretty when you cried."

What did he say?

"You're so pretty when you cry."

Had Daniel never seen me cry? Almost two years in Italy, without my family, with no girlfriends, fired from a big job, in not such a copacetic relationship—and my lover had never seen me cry?

Jesus Christ and his foreskin too.

And that's when it hit me. I had spent so much time perfecting the packaging of my romantic entanglements that I never allowed myself to just be a girl, hoping to settle down and struggling with my situation. This prism of grace and resilience and what-doesn't-kill-you-makes-you-stronger that I had scripted for myself? Toxic positivity. And no longer my truth. It was time to confront my own bullshit. I was circling the drain. Fragile and fearful. All out of inner spirit and je ne sais quos. I wanted to curl up in a ball of shame and blame and hate, and not *let it go* but let it rip. Because I'd romantically bottomed out. Love sucked. And I was done pretending otherwise.

No. This was not the breakup I would survive with style. This was the breakup that would break me open and let me ache and bleed and scream for as long as I wanted to. I would not get tipsy with happily married friends cheers-ing to my freedom. I would not publish witty things about getting over him so I could get under someone else. There would be no *soldiering on* in a cute sweat suit embroidered with *Sunny Days*. I would stand in the cold, mean storm, shivering. I would grieve the ugly-sexy couple we were. I would regret ever stepping foot in Italy. I would feel terrified for my future. I would feel immensely sorry for myself and the merciless deck of love cards I was dealt. I would pick at all the scabs of my past. I would mourn for the kids I might never have. I would turn my back on men and sex and relationships, and pray to never endure any of it again.

Daniel would be my last bad breakup—I promised myself that much. But he was also likely to be my last love story, too. Because I was officially done. *This was as far as I could go.*

After settling back into Brooklyn, with my mind in a very twisted and negative headspace, a package arrived in the mail from somewhere far off. Daniel, whom I never spoke to again after I left Italy, had mailed me a few of the things I'd left behind. A small copper pot. A Prada key chain, from the outlet. The silver basket from Giacamo, my bike.

Floating loose in the box was also a scrap of paper, with a scribbled note that read: *Have a nice life, Bella.*

All I could do was try to remember at least one way to say *Screw you* in Italian.

eight

The Life-Changing Cappuccino

Amanda Freeman blew into City Bakery in the Flatiron District of New York City wearing a wide-brimmed fedora and massive starlet sunglasses, with a fresh blowout that smelled like apricots and figs, and asked me one simple question: "Do you have ten thousand bucks?"

I was on a blind friend date with Amanda, the first Single Mom by Choice I'd ever met in real life. Her older sister, Danyelle, was one of my best friends, and though Danyelle and I had known each other for several years, Amanda was always some intangible, ultra-successful force of nature I'd only heard intimidating stories about. She was a fitness and wellness entrepreneur, but the kind who would *never* say namaste, and here she was in real life, in Rag & Bone, in her first trimester, emboldening *me* on exactly how to get pregnant without a penis. This was unbelievable.

And I did have ten thousand bucks! Not a penny more, especially after my six-dollar cappuccino at City Bakery, but I did have that much in savings from Airbnb-ing my apartment while I was in Italy.

"Good. Then you can at least get started," Amanda said.

"Really? That's all I need?"

"Yeah. Assuming you don't have any major fertility issues, you'll be fine. I don't know how you'll survive with a kid afterward, but you probably have enough to get pregnant."

This, I found astonishing. If I was really going to have a baby on my own, money was not the ultimate deciding factor. This was an emotional and spiritual journey, not a financial one. However, I needed to know if I could even afford to *think* about it, logistically. I mean, I always assumed alternative baby-making was an option for rich girls only. Didn't fertility stuff cost hundreds of thousands of dollars? And yet Amanda said I had just enough to get pregnant. And that was nothing short of amazing to me. As the kids with better egg reserves than me might say, it was *like whoa.*

Amanda herself was wealthy, but she was self-made, down-to-earth, and not spoiled at all. She "got" that I was a freelance writer without loaded parents, who made about $50K in a good year, and could never afford anything luxurious like a "night nurse," or even a car service to the delivery room. Sure, I had it much, much easier than many women who might aspire to motherhood—a job that would allow me to stay home and work; an able body; the most supportive family, who all lived within a one-mile radius of me, including my own parents, who literally lived in the same building, just down the hall—and I had profound gratitude for all those advantages. However, I also had abysmal health insurance, unpredictable freelance assignments that could evaporate at any moment without notice, and definitely not a second bedroom or a nursery (now that's hilarious!).

Fertility costs aside, I knew nothing else about the "artificial in-semination" process other than that I cringed at the term. It sounded so clinical and cold. But with the dazzling Amanda at the wheel, all that went out the window. A black Porsche window. She was so cool and direct and nonperformative about it all, and she made the whole pregnancy prospect feel so accessible: *Make an appointment with this doctor . . . buy a membership with this sperm bank . . . make sure you bring a friend for this appointment because it's really uncomfortable, etc.*

I couldn't believe the conversation was even happening, let alone that it all felt so manageable. It was so much more "pinch me" than "kill me," and I wanted nothing more than to keep listening. After all, this was, I am almost positive, the first time in my life I had reached out and asked someone for help. With anything. Let alone *this,* which was everything. And my goodness, did I pick the right time and the right person. Because—on the record—this was the talk that changed my life. Without taking off her oversized shades, with the tiniest crumb of a pretzel croissant accessorizing her cheekbone, Amanda Freeman gave me permission to have a baby on my own.

But what I appreciated even more than that was the sexy-ass confidence she brought to that white marble café table.

Speaking of white marble café tables, I'd been back from Rome for a few months. At first, I retreated and sulked. I bought a mug that read *I wonder if life smokes after it fucks me.* I didn't try to "rally" or construct some sham of a silver lining. The breakup with Dan-iel had drained me of everything flirtatious or vivacious I had left inside. My inner flame was out, and I wasn't sure if I'd ever be lit from within again. I mean, *how many breakups can somebody go through before they are officially broken?* Rome left me without any romantic gas in the tank, not one single drop, and that was my reality. In love, I could not win.

But what's also my reality was that I don't particularly enjoy being sad. It is not my natural baseline; melancholy is too boring after a while. So one night, unable to stay withdrawn from the natural pleasures of being a human being in the world, I strapped myself back into the rocket ship and decided to fix up my one wild and precious life once and for all. I marched myself to the bathroom mirror, looked deep into my own watery brown eyes, and demanded to know, "What is it you want, Alyssa? What do you want to do next? What will make you happy? *What. Will. Make. You. Happy.*"

I allowed myself to respond with anything that surfaced. Whatever rose from my heart would be okay with me. There would be no edits, no judgment, no right or wrong. If the answer was an entire carrot cake, I would take myself to Betty Bakery on Atlantic Avenue and fork it in until I couldn't take another bite. If the answer was to jump off the Brooklyn Bridge, I would take myself straight to a psychiatric facility. But the answer was neither as light as cream cheese frosting nor as dark as killing myself. The answer was clear, and striking, and adamant. *Motherhood.* All I wanted was motherhood. It was time.

Half a second after my epiphany, I ran to my phone and called my parents, then conferenced in my newly married and pregnant sister, and breathlessly asked, "Hey, guys, quick question. How would you guys feel if I had a baby on my own?" The call instantly erupted in uncontrollable cheer and celebration. The whole family spent hours and hours screaming and howling for joy. My mom's only pressing question was "What took you so long?"

So yes, hard yes, I was ready to pursue motherhood. And I wanted to do it alone. This was not a sign of defeat; this was my core truth. Viscerally, deep in my soul, I was not interested in searching for, or involving, or wasting my time with, any man along the way. What got me into this mess was not going to get me out of it. It's not that I had turned into a raging man hater, per se. I just didn't want another difficult man—since I was allergic to all the nice and easy ones—on this journey with me. I really, truly, fundamentally did not. They could all watch from the cheap seats.

The decision felt unquestionably right. As far as I was concerned, no man meant no drama, and no drama meant no combat. But . . . I was not so naive to think that any of this would be completely conflict-free. In the beginning, if I'm being completely up-front, my primary hesitation was about image. There was a small yet disquieting voice in my head that was insecure about what people would think. Would friends, colleagues, readers, or future flings think I was too flawed to have a baby with a partner? Would they wonder how appalling or annoying or psychotic I must really be behind the scenes? It seemed like everyone could find their "forever love"—except me. Did that make me pathetic? I shuddered to think about all the gossip, even though I generally didn't bother with self-consciousness. I always said the single best thing my prideful mother did for me was show, by example, how to not give a shit about what anybody thinks of you. "Oh, who the hell cares?!" I could hear her hooting. However, any behind-my-back small talk that I imagined, about my *own womb* of all things, felt explicitly hard to brush off. Could I get past the inevitable whispers? I wasn't sure.

But then I absorbed more of Amanda. As she inhaled her pastry while answering a call from one of her business partners and simultaneously putting in a bid on a bigger downtown loft, I stared at her the way you would the *Mona Lisa* at the Louvre. If the *Mona Lisa* was, like, one of the enviable authors of *How to Be Parisian Wherever You Are*. Amanda was tan and beautiful and powerful. She was only a few weeks pregnant herself, and her body was gorgeous. She was impossibly chic. And very busy. And intelligent. And lovely. Anyone would want to date her. *I* wanted to date her! What I gleaned from my laser-focused observance of Amanda across that table reframed how I looked at the Single Mother by Choice movement forever. Because this was not a woman who couldn't get a man. This was a woman who did not *need* a man. And as I soaked that in, on that unforgettable fall afternoon, my life was transformed forever.

I was all in.

"Keep me posted," she said, scooping up her Hermès shoulder bag, overflowing gym tote, and monogrammed laptop sleeve before running off to a secret club for high-stake female investors, and definitely not a nap. "By winter, you could be *preggers*." We both felt silly about the silly word, but also completely delighted by it. We tightly hugged goodbye, and I sat back down smiling so hard that I had to hide my stupid face in my hands.

On the F train home, divorced from any lingering inhibition, I started writing what would become my "coming out" article for *New York* magazine titled "I Love Men, But I'm Thinking of Having a Baby Without One."

My essay was published a week later. Within a few hours after it was posted, the story was consumed by thousands of readers, and I was totally at peace with that. Actually, I was thrilled. I had cracked the code on how to have a baby while still being me, and all it took was a painfully honest conversation with myself and a little push from a great woman standing in my corner. That in itself felt revelatory and worth sharing with other single and possibly scared women, looking for a rope to hold on to.

Of course, the comments below my essay were bound to be atrocious. In my experience, any piece about a bold woman, or any woman with her own electric spark, yields the meanest trollwork of all. It's almost an insult if it doesn't. That's why if there's any rule I follow in life it's to *never* read the comments. They're simply ludicrous. This time, though, in the spirit of IDGAF, I took a peek. Sure enough, for every three *You rock!!!* comments, there were dozens of versions of *You idiotic, selfish woman* and *No one will want you now.* Someone—somewhere online—even wrote, *Have fun dying alone!*

I didn't love it, but I had to take it on the chin, and maybe even learn something. Maybe these would be some of the typical reactions I'd have to face as a Single Mom by Choice—not just by creeps jerking off in their mothers' basements while selling half-eaten cans of garbanzo beans on Craigslist but by distant relatives at family reunions and random friends on WhatsApp—and I guess it was good to prepare myself. My choice would not sit right with everyone, not just the villains online.

As the wonderful *and* wretched comments streamed in under the article, so did the emails in my inbox. These notes were from real readers using their real names, expressing heartfelt support and solidarity for my journey and overall personhood. The letters were from upbeat, well-adjusted, fully functional humans who spent time seeking out my email address simply to say, *You got this, girl.* Or, *Thank you for making me feel less alone.* Or, *I sent this to my best friend who's struggling with the same issues and we finally had an open conversation about everything.*

Those notes, which have never stopped trickling into my inbox since, became my north stars. And like the illuminating Amanda was for me, I started feeling like someday I could be a valuable source for women who did not swiftly get married and have kids, or who never found love that lasted, or who only found love that hurt; for the women who exclusively had casual sex, or no sex, or nothing that ever fell under the category of an understandable romantic relationship; for the women left behind in the rom-coms and the sitcoms; for those who needed to hear a serious promise from a real person that there is more than one way to design a happy life.

As far as me actually *becoming* a Single Mother by Choice—putting my money where my, um, uterus was—I still had a long and winding road ahead, not just up and down my fallopian tubes but through some challenging obstacles of the mind and heart. But never again would I waste my time worrying about any shit talk. And honestly, there was barely any. Not from anybody who mattered, at least. The truth was, I never experienced so much empathy and generosity in my entire life as I did when I told the world that I was hardwired to be a mom, that I did not need a man, that I wasn't going to wait anymore, and that it was absolutely *not* open for discussion.

Oh, and regarding dying alone? That's where the dear troll covered in Doritos dust went wrong. Because if all went well, I would never be alone again.

nine

Dr. Grifo

I lit a leather-scented candle, turned up the National, poured a big glass of tempranillo, and logged on to California Cryobank.

CCB was one of the Amanda-approved sperm banks, and when I found out the vice president of the company liked media attention, I knew he'd respond well to an email from me. After some friendly back-and-forth, he gladly sent me a "press code," which meant I could browse the site for free, with VIP access to all the accoutrements, like recorded interviews with the sperm donors as adults and bonus pictures of them as kids. Of all the swag and perks of my work—including a Cartier bangle and an afternoon with Tom Brady—this one, unquestionably, dominated everything.

Believe it or not, swiping through the sperm donor profiles— perusing their baby pictures and learning basic info about their in- terests and personality types—was much more scintillating than any of the online dating I'd done. I mean, each guy presented a totally different narrative and story line to me—and unlike most of my exes, any of them would theoretically get me pregnant! While many women find this part of the process daunting, for me it was a creative exercise in imagination and possibility. Which is also to say, after deciding to have a baby on my own, I got my inner love 'n light back.

Did I want my baby to look like a Shelasky, or was it better to mix up the gene pool? Was it important that they had athleticism in their DNA? What about a knack for foreign languages, or engineering? Would my baby be a Taylor Kitsch clone? How 'bout Orlando Bloom? I obviously reveled in the "celebrity look-alike" feature the most. When I asked the sperm bank people why anyone would want sperm that looked like, say, a young Ray Romano (no offense, Ray), they reminded me that some couples struggling with fertility want sperm that resembles their actual partner. Oh, right.

While I basked in the prospect of having a baby with Mr. Emerald Eyes or the premed student who double majored in classical music, every few donors, my mind would drift to a less wondrous side of things. I had narrowed the search down to "open donors," which meant my child could get the donor's personal information when he or she turned eighteen. This option brought me a little peace of mind. Though I never worried about myself as a future single mother, I did worry about the happy heart of my future child. My son or daughter would not have a father. There would be no dad. He wouldn't be some deadbeat in the Florida Keys, or remarried to a spinning instructor out east. He would not exist. That's not just tough, that's potentially traumatic, and I was already overwhelmingly protective of my little one's tender soul. Would their fatherlessness haunt them? Would it torture them? Was this whole thing supremely selfish of me? What would my kid do on Father's Day when all the other children were finger-painting Father's Day cards, or if the preschool had some terrible, tone-deaf program like Doughnuts with Daddy? How would I skim over Papa Bear in the Berenstain Bears, and mute out Daddy Pig in *Peppa Pig*? Would my son or daughter go through life feeling weird and alienated just because I had to be so radical and edgy?

But then I'd think: Well, maybe we could go to the South of France every Father's Day. That could be our tradition. And maybe no one in Brooklyn has both a mom and a dad anymore—"normal" is no longer a thing, right? Maybe Doughnuts with Daddy is just some uncool suburban bullshit, way out of our orbit. Maybe we'd only read kid books about being different. Maybe I'd write kid books about being different. Because we'd definitely love that about ourselves, and we'd never want to hide it. Mama and kiddo against the world—that would be us. My child would always know how badly I wanted them. That I moved mountains to bring them into this world only to give them the most beautiful life. And even if that was not enough, I knew without one iota of a doubt that my child would have unconditional love every single second of the day, and all throughout the night, until the day I died, and then beamed down from heaven, and that would be plenty to get us through the rough stuff. And then I'd re-harness my grit and return to the Ryan Seacrest doppelganger, and the soccer player with a sensitive side, and the academic who moonlights at comedy clubs. And I'd get excited again.

Speaking of the finest of male specimens: Dr. James Grifo at NYU is largely regarded as the best fertility doctor in New York, if not the country, and I was set on becoming his patient. So once again, I pulled some strings. My friend at CNN, Jen, made a call for me, and told his people I was a "big writer" at *New York* magazine. His assistant contacted me for an appointment a few days later. Turns out, he totally would have seen me without all the bells and whistles, but I like telling the story with some dramatic flair.

The waiting room at NYU felt like a welcoming enough conference room at a hotel. Lots of light brown furniture. Reticent energy. Rather clammy. It held a random assortment of women and couples, all spread out and sitting noiselessly and reservedly, sipping various bodega coffees and teas. My mom came with me to the first appointment and sat quietly beside me, holding my hand. We both looked around, inconspicuously nosy as always. There were a lot of Orthodox Jews, which neither of us were expecting. There were several white women in their forties who all looked like they worked in book publishing and were still despondent about Hillary Clinton's presidential loss and had calicos named Sadie. And there were a handful of cute "regular" couples who I assumed were from New Jersey or Long Island, anxiously fidgeting in their seats while murmuring about where the car was parked. No one moved around or intermingled. There was no exchange of fertility struggles. No ovulation updates. No endometriosis chatter. Just library voices and oak side tables, with stacks of magazines, filled with flowery articles probably written by me.

There was only one thing that *most* of us women had in common. It was the thing that none of us had: our youth. We were not the generation of women who liked to get slapped in the face during sex. Nor were we the girls who posted selfies of our luscious side boobs with a *might delete later* hashtag. We did not know the difference be-

tween Zayn Malik and Harry Styles. We didn't TikTok or Nae Nae or
even Cha Cha Matcha. We wouldn't all get pregnant. Many would be
in for the battle of a lifetime. Some would have chemical pregnancies, most would have miscarriages, and a few would need to termi-
nate late-term because their babies would be born terminally sick,
if even alive. We were older, grown-ass women who were there to
fight tough for our motherhood, and I was proud to sit among them.

Someone in scrubs called my name and my mother and I gasped.
Before I stood up, I kissed her on the cheek and softly said, "I'll go
myself. You stay here." If I was self-reliant enough to have a baby
alone, I could get through my first fertility appointment solo too.

As the assistant ushered me toward Dr. Grifo's doors, one part
of me wanted to bow down at the doctor's feet and the other part
wanted to shit my pants. I was nervous. It was like, *This is the moment
I've waited my whole life for* and *This is the moment I never wanted to see
happen* both coming together at the exact same time, like a big cos-
mic joke. The assistant opened the amber entranceway to his den-
like office, and there he was: the great man who was going to get me
pregnant. He was at once smoldering and dead serious.

We introduced ourselves. And because I didn't know what to
say next, I landed on the thing that always saves me, the thing that
recalibrates my equilibrium, makes me feel good about myself, and
makes me sound cool: my reliable savior, my work.

"So, yeah, I write about women's issues for 'The Cut' at *New York*
magazine . . . and I'm probably going to be writing about coming
to see you, too! All good things. But just so you know."

Considering there was no official assignment, and I had nothing
to write about at this point, it was a slight exaggeration. And as

per usual, I came in too hot. Grifo, who was preoccupied looking through my files, didn't even flinch.

While I was occasionally—though not nearly enough—writing for "The Cut," *New York* magazine's most desirable online section for "Fashion, Beauty, Politics, Sex and Celebrity," I was mostly considered a food writer over there because of my cheffy memoir. Though it wasn't the work I necessarily wanted to be doing, writing about food had its perks. I became intimately familiar (sometimes too intimately) with all the high-end restaurants, cheap eats, food trucks, and secret gems around America. My social life consisted of going to swanky restaurant openings, food festivals, meals with controversial restaurant demigods, and precious tasting menus run by eccentric chefs who considered themselves artists but were usually just sociopaths. Though I generally found restaurant culture to be self-important, self-indulgent, and on the side of super-boring, I was good at my job. I could spar with almost anybody about the best cold sesame noodles or omakase sushi or cozy first date spot. And any of the above was usually a stellar conversation starter. So, why not double down and give it a shot here?

"But I mostly write about good restaurants," I continued, hoping Grifo would bite this time. "Need help with any reservations?"

A misfire.

All he did was take out a pen.

"You're thirty-seven. Do you have a partner? A boyfriend? A girlfriend?" he asked, straight to the point. He was a no-nonsense man. A classy man. The kind of man, I'm assuming, who is disgusted by pumpkin-scented candles and East Coast skiing and gerrymandering.

"I have a lot of boyfriends," I said, just provocatively enough to make it weird. Grifo grinned to be polite. Was I trying to seduce my fertility doctor? Kind of. I mean, not in a sexual way, but I wanted him to like me. And to work extra-hard to get me pregnant because he was extra-invested in me. And maybe he'd also knock off a blood work bill or two. Would that be so wrong?

"Sorry. Um . . ." I continued, closing my legs. "No. I want to use a sperm donor."

"Smart," he said. "At your age, if you know you want kids, and you can handle all the emotional and financial responsibilities, you should go for it."

Totally. Great minds. And great fucking hands . . .

"Did you pick the donor?"

I told him I had narrowed it down to a few interesting prospects and was having a donor-viewing party with my family later that night. Knowing he was probably Italian, with a last name like Grifo, I made sure to add that I was going to make an "orecchiette" pasta dish inspired by my time in Puglia to accompany the experience.

"Little ears," I said, translating the word while caressing my ear, like an asshole.

A pause.

"Puglia's nice," he complied, graciously.

A small victory.

Grifo felt satisfied with our preliminary session, but not before adding that I'd need to pass a psych test—*standard,* he insisted, but I wasn't so sure. Then he suggested we move to the next room for my physical examination. I was not expecting this. Suddenly I felt extremely ashamed. Not for being a romantically bankrupt and emotionally adrift woman who was having a baby without a man but for not shaving and exfoliating my legs for this foxy fertility luminary who deserved better than my dry, dead skin with winter itch.

As Grifo brought in a nurse and got organized around the medical table I was lying on, I tried to make some more small talk. I half-jokingly asked him if all his patients were in love with him. (They were, I already knew that from Jen at CNN.) To which he changed the subject to genetic testing. I'd need to schedule that appointment next. Then I asked him how many babies of former patients were running around New York with names like Grif. He bashfully said there were a few. Then he started probing around. I may or may not have pretended that we were in a fetish porn.

The porno came to a screeching halt when Grifo said, "Do you know you have fibroids, Alyssa?"

Not only did I not know, but I had no idea what fibroids were. In an instant, the tools felt colder and harsher inside my body. He explained that fibroids are generally noncancerous, and oftentimes nonissues, but because I had several large ones in all the wrong places, he was concerned. He said the fibroids were so big that he worried they might interfere with me having a healthy pregnancy. From what my brain could compute, it sounded like the fibroids could crowd the womb and prevent a baby from growing or surviving in there. "If we can even get you pregnant," he explained, "I'm not sure you will *stay* pregnant."

Grifo's style was straightforward, and he didn't mince words or sugarcoat anything, and that's what I liked about him, but it was a lot to process at once. I had no idea I had these repellent fibroid chunks lurking inside me, though in hindsight, there was always an odd, throbbing sensation when I ovulated. I half-heartedly assumed it was just my uterus saying, "Knock me up already! Knock me up already!" As this new information sank in, my mind went dark for a minute, and I wondered if the fibroids were grown from the particles of my romantic pain, where the toxicity of my exes had been stored, and where love's ruins and disappointments implanted themselves, only to rot inside me.

Grifo said I should consider getting them surgically removed— not a small surgery, he warned—and he referred me to a specialist for a second opinion. Then he left the room for a Hasid named Hadassah, but not without a warm and caring goodbye. I glumly got myself dressed, throwing the sass in the trash, and went looking for my mom in the waiting room.

When I saw her, I was too shell-shocked to say anything. I didn't want to cry, either. I had promised myself that if I was embarking on this Single Mom by Choice journey, I would remain brave and unbreakable the whole way through. Once again, there would be *nothing* I couldn't handle. And this was my first test.

Out on the street, walking with my shoulders slumped forward, I tried to plainly and unemotionally explain the fibroid discoveries to her. She looked crushed. It was a look I've rarely seen before on my mother's pathologically hopeful face. She asked, in the gentlest way possible, if the fibroids were a product of my age. With a tremor in my voice, I confessed that I had asked the doctor the same question, and the answer was probably yes.

"I waited too long, Mom," I said, my head hung low with indignity. *I waited too long.*

ten

Did You Bring a Vibrator?

The Fancy Fibroid Surgeon Man agreed that I should get the little fuckers surgically removed.

He was absolutely convinced that I would never get pregnant with those uterine terrorists growing on the vines of my insides. "No chance," he said bleakly, adding that even if I did get pregnant, "You would one hundred percent miscarry." He also told me that surgery would delay my pregnancy plans for about a year, and not a day less. And then he explained, without an ounce of charisma, that the potential scar tissue could prevent a healthy pregnancy altogether, in all new ways.

Neither option—trying to get pregnant with fibroids lurking everywhere or enduring a major surgery to get them out—could guarantee a healthy, perfect, risk-free pregnancy. But there's no such guarantee. What no one tells you when you're dreaming of motherhood is that it's all one big long shot. Every prenatal appointment is another chance to find out more unthinkable news. Conceiving—and delivering—a healthy baby is a goddamn miracle no matter what your circumstances are.

My mother, who was back to her indefatigable self, continued to remind me that "Surgeons just want to cut!" and that the Fancy Fibroid Surgeon Man "sounded like a moron!" (Considering she used to *pay* me and my sister to sit on the Columbia medical school steps and pretend to be lost so that we could catch and trap a nice Jewish doctor, this was an interesting pivot.) Suffice to say, she firmly believed I should get pregnant ASAP and let nothing get in our way. After reviewing and rereviewing multiple scans and measurements of the fibroids with Dr. Grifo and other obstetric experts, there was no clear-cut answer on which road to take. All I could do was go with my gut. And my gut said to try to conceive, and hope like hell. Moving forward, the fibroids would be nothing more than a footnote in our story. The decision was made.

Grifo respected my choice to try for a pregnancy. And we immediately proceeded with a meticulous schedule of blood work and other mandatory tests and appointments. I've never followed any instructions, directions, or rules so carefully. Had I been so obedient and driven with anything else in my life, I would be a bestselling author with an oceanfront beach house in Malibu right now, a chopped chicken salad with green goddess dressing would be on its way, and I'd get a facial massage every single night *in bed,* like I once read in *Bazaar* Sonia Rykiel does. Oh well.

A few weeks later it was time for my first, and hopefully only, IUI. The procedure was scheduled for early January, a Sunday at 11:30 A.M. But on Friday morning there was bigger pregnancy news. My sister,

Rachel, had gone into labor! And being the crazy close family that we are—emphasis on "crazy"—my parents and I were at the hospital with her, and my brother-in-law, for at least thirty-six hours in advance of the main event, even though we really only needed to be there for the last two. Charles Hunter Karasik was born at 4:28 A.M. on Sunday. He was the first baby in our family, and needless to say, our magnificent prince. I was honored to be there to welcome him into this world, but I was also deranged from exhaustion.

What did this mean for my IUI? Well, I essentially zombie-walked through the snow directly from my sister's hospital room at Mount Sinai to my procedure room at NYU, a couple miles away, and by the time I got there, I was a little spun-out. I remember passing Barbara Corcoran of *Shark Tank* somewhere along the way. She was sitting alone at a Subway and contentedly wolfing down a six-foot-long sandwich. It looked like tuna fish. And I thought to myself, *See? That's why she's rich.* A sucker like me woulda been at Balthazar.

Still buzzing from the birth of my nephew and physically spent, I was not exactly in a state of wholeness for the appointment. From the minute I checked in, the entire scene felt asynchronous. Nothing was special or meaningful or choreographed just right, and I knew the IUI was not going to work. I just knew it. And maybe my futile attitude played a part in the negative pregnancy test two weeks later, but my maternal instincts were already switched on and they had whispered to me, "Not this time, honey." I didn't blame the fibroids, and I definitely didn't blame my super-delicious and surprisingly furry new nephew. It just wasn't meant to be that month, and I didn't give the non-pregnancy any more power than that.

Four weeks later my mom came to the next IUI with me. I woke up feeling feverish. Feverish in a *good* way. Adventurous. Sensuous. I'm sorry to use "horny" and my mother in the same paragraph, but: I was insanely fucking horny. Like, I was in heat. I felt soft and round and ripe and womanly. I felt . . . I suppose the word is "fertile." Doggedly fertile.

It was an icy and iridescent February morning and freezing cold out, and the whole twenty-minute walk from the subway station to NYU felt pixelated and enhanced, like it was all happening inside a sparkly montage written and directed by Sofia Coppola.

We were taken to a nice big room way down the hall, past the blood work stations and the scales and blood pressure machines and the small bathrooms filled with pee cups and Sharpies for writing your name on them. Dr. Grifo never did the actual inseminations, but I passed him in the hallway and it was like a mini–spa trip for my soul. He gave me an encouraging wink, and all my important body parts felt even tinglier.

In the room, naked but for a paper gown, a matter-of-fact nurse named either Mary or Linda told me to lie back and relax. My mom, my most devoted coconspirator as always, sat beside me and took my hand. I put my feet in the stirrups—never exactly Shakespeare in the Park—and closed my eyes. I could feel my mother pressing all her hope and faith through her soft palm into my sweaty flesh. As Mary or Linda inserted and maneuvered her wand and administered her spermly magic, I tried to dissociate from reality, and go to a higher place, and invite the magic in.

When the procedure was over, the nurse said I could lie there and rest for a few minutes, to let everything "settle." Before she left, I touched her wrist and thanked her for helping me start a family. "Good luck," she said, neither here nor there. After she left the room, I told my mom I wanted to be still and mellow, and meditate for a few minutes, with my legs up in the air so the sperm could swim like they mean it. But she had another idea in mind.

"Did you bring a vibrator?" she whispered, not quietly.

"What? Mom! No! Why would I . . ."

She had read in a magazine that a woman should have an orgasm after an IUI, to simulate "real sex," and to enhance the flow of things. Nonscientifically speaking, it kind of actually made sense, and I'm not just saying that because I probably wrote the piece. But still! There was no way.

Gross Mom Factor aside, my vibrator had been dead for at least two years. The fact that I couldn't find the motivation to locate the right charger in the last 730 days, and that it was probably shoved in a drawer with busted headphones, loose peanut M&M's, and random stray earrings even though I don't have my ears pierced, was not a great look in terms of my domesticity meter. But neurotic parents make neurotic kids, right?

My lack of a sex toy did not matter to my mother as she folded herself into an en suite medical closet, yelling at me to get off "the old-fashioned way!"

Now. We are a ride-or-die family, and my mom and I were born troublemakers, but her asking me to rub one out so that I could give her a second grandchild was too much, even for me.

"Mom. Get out of the supply closet now," I implored, not hushed at all, waving my hands frantically. "Seriously. Get out of there! They'll be furious if they walk in here!"

Did she listen? Oh hell no.

However, I will say, her antics did more good than harm.

Because this imagery of my mother, crouched down under some white uniforms, shoved between an ultrasound machine and a big box of syringes, the arm of her bright coral DKNY sweatshirt covering her gleeful eyes, screaming, "Think of Dr. Grifo! Think of Dr. Grifo!" was the best thing I ever saw.

And suddenly I was laughing hysterically. We laughed as I got myself dressed and as I paid the otherwise unfunny IUI bill. We laughed on the F train home, my head on her shoulder in between the giggle fits. We laughed telling the story to everyone we encountered, the more inappropriate the person, the better. And we laughed ourselves to sleep that night. And I for one believe that our overflowing and unbound joy made all the difference.

Because seven or eight weeks later, we were back in that room, and my sister was with us this time. Dr. Grifo cruised in (if he only knew any of the above) and squirted some cold jelly on my stomach. I already knew I was pregnant from the seventy pregnancy tests I had taken in the last month, and the seventeen falafels that I had already inhaled out of starvation. But I also knew it was early and I was old and there were fibroids, and that there were no promises that the pregnancy would stick, or that the baby even had a heartbeat.

"Your baby has a heartbeat," said Dr. Grifo in his calm, steady tone, but this time with a faint tinge of *really freakin' psyched for you.* "A strong, healthy heartbeat."

He gave me an estimated due date: October 30, 2015.

"Is it going to be okay, Dr. Grifo?" I asked, with my heart in my throat. My sister was bawling. My mother was beaming. Grifo had a twinkle in his eye and finally broke into a big, substantial smile. The smile I had been waiting for. "All I can say is: you're in the game."

eleven

A Love Letter to My Anonymous Sperm Donor

Dear Vince Vaughn,

I call you Vince Vaughn because he was one of your celebrity look-alikes, and he's allegedly part Middle Eastern, which you are too. And, hey, who doesn't feel happy thinking of Vince Vaughn?

It's tricky to write this letter, because you're anonymous and I want to respect your privacy and the privacy of my future daughter (who I've started to refer to as "my little fig"). So without saying too much . . . there are so many things that amaze me about you. Your worldly upbringing; all the languages you speak; your creativity, spirituality, skills; all your heroes; your struggles. This might sound strange—but I brag about you to my family and friends. I do! Even though you are essentially a complete stranger. . . .

In fact, Vince, I say this with kindness and affection—and I'm sure the feeling is mutual—I never need to meet you. You are not my soul mate. I do not consider you my daughter's father. You will only materialize into a real, living, breathing creature if she is curious about you someday. And I pray for those curiosities to live inside her in a warm and safe place. If and when she's ready to find out more, I will be right there beside her with full support. But that will be many years from now, if ever.

I don't know why you donated sperm. From what I've researched, men usually do it for one of three reasons: money, kindness, or ego. Either they need cash and this seems a lot more fun than sitting in some depressing office; or they're predisposed to acts of paying it forward and want to help families in need; or they think their genes are so exceptional and superior that it's their moral obligation to spread them all across the universe so that humankind is taller, kinder, smarter, funnier, and all around more genetically blessed thanks to their contribution. I have a feeling you're a hybrid of all three, and I am totally okay with any of it.

I saved a black-and-white photograph of you as a young child on my phone. You were born in another country; I don't know which one, but this photo had to be taken there because it feels so otherworldly. You look like you were around five years old. It lives in my Favorites. I often look at the photo on the subway with quiet delight. Tired working moms peek over my shoulder as if I'm staring at my own young son. They sympathetically smile at me, and I look at them, like, I know. Isn't he something?

Once, in LA, I thought I saw you at a bohemian coffee shop. (Not the actor, the real you.) I don't actually know what you look like beyond age eight or so, but this man was exactly how I imagined you as a grown-up. Spying from my little wicker table, I froze in my seat. I know that I froze because I wanted to snap a picture of you as proof, in case it was only an invented memory, but my arms were too immobilized to lift my phone. Even if I could have moved my body, I had no words, and I probably didn't want to say anything anyway. Because if the lovely man drinking the flat white was you, VV, I knew that it was better for you to exist purely as fantasy. At least for now.

Here's what I want to say to you simply by virtue of putting it out in the universe: Thank you. Of all the men I've trusted thus far, you are the only one who has never disappointed me. You helped me get pregnant when I was out of faith and strength. You provided me with the most important gift of one's lifetime: a child. Nothing can ever be more sacred than that.

This might be the first time that anyone has ever felt this way about an anonymous sperm donor whom she hopes to never know or see with her own eyes, but here it goes: My dear, I will love you forever.

Alyssa

twelve

Echo Park

I was eight months pregnant and hauling ass around Hollywood. There were two scripted television shows in development about my life. One producer had suggested Lake Bell play me; the other was imagining Mila Kunis. And as if all that wasn't trippy enough, I also had a pussy hound of a new boyfriend texting for pictures of my huge, uncontainable, and ever-growing cantaloupe tits.

It's true. When I wasn't busy growing a human being inside my body, these were the days that I was also attempting to break into the entertainment industry. I didn't plan to rev up my professional drive at the exact same time that I was finally attempting to "nest," but I am a devout believer in "when opportunity knocks." And that's what happened. Opportunity knocked, and there I was, with my own milky knockers, trying to make it rain.

The first show was about that inglorious *See Alyssa Date* blog. The same producers who wanted to make a series about it ten years ago were still flirting with the concept. Every year or so, they'd check in with me to see if I'd warmed to the idea. This year, given that I was pregnant and needed money, I was finally motivated to jump on board. These guys were huge TV show creators in Hollywood now, and it was a no-brainer to align myself with them if I was craving any modicum of success, even if I still hated thinking about that blog.

The other show was about my decision to have a baby on my own and raise her alongside my "eclectic and eccentric village." This one was put into motion by my good friend Todd Spiewak and his husband, Jim Parsons, the star of *The Big Bang Theory,* who were starting their own production company and wanted the *Untitled Alyssa Single Mom Show* to be the first project they went out with. The characters were closely based on my real family. We imagined Bette Midler playing my mother, and Alan Alda playing my dad. I cosigned on that casting right away.

To boil down the grind, albeit a glamorous grind, that is TV development: there are constant calls and meetings and drafts and pitches for months or maybe years, with zero guarantee of anything ever happening. For nobodies like me, you only make money if your show actually makes it on air. And statistically speaking, that's probably not going to happen. You have a better chance of winning the lottery than getting your series on air, even with A-list celebrities like Jim Parsons attached. It's pure masochism really, TV development. There's so much pressure and so much work, and you literally don't see a penny unless lightning strikes. But hey. I was a dreamer. You couldn't last a day in Hollywood if you weren't. Plus, if either of my shows *did* make it, I would earn hundreds of thousands of dollars and become a big-time TV writer, and as a future single mom with about three thousand dollars left in the bank, my thirst and ambition were at an all-time high. Thus, barefoot and pregnant, tiptoeing through the tulips, I was not. This was a time of pure, uncut hustle.

But what's much more interesting than any of that industry bullshit is that while I was out pregnant and working like an animal in LA, I also had a fabulous horndog of a boyfriend there.

Ross and I met just before I got pregnant. I was in Los Angeles getting those TV deals on track and also scouting guys online for Shelley, my best friend in West Hollywood. Whenever I came to town, I'd take over her Tinder account and initiate some high-level, witty banter for her because flirting is my superpower. After vetting Ross's pictures (grizzly and attractive) and his personality (outgoing and libidinous) and doing a quick Googlestalk that led to photos of him performing with the National, the only cool band I knew and loved, I initiated a conversation on Shelley's behalf. It went something like this:

Me: So you're a musician . . . that means you're either some irresistible train wreck or stone-cold sober. Which one is it?

Ross: Hahaha. Three years sober. But can't I be sober *and* irresistible?

Me: Definitely. And good for you. Did you ever read the book *I Don't Care About Your Band*?

Ross: Nope, but it sounds good. Did you write it?

Me: I should have. (I'm a writer.)

Ross: Writers are so sexy.

Me: Full disclosure, I'm only swiping for my best friend.
This is her account. She is hot + v. successful.

Ross: Ah, shame. Don't you think we have chemistry?

Me: Honey, you don't want to associate with the guys I have
chemistry with.

Ross: LOL. What's your story?

Me: I'm single, but I'm trying to have a baby on my own.
Hoping to be pregnant by next month. That's all I really
care about right now.

Ross: Wow. That's awesome. Can I take you to dinner?
Please? We won't have any chemistry. Promise.

It took a few minutes of consideration. I was still in something
of a romantic hiatus. Dating had been completely off my radar in-
sofar as I hadn't thought about men since leaving Rome, which was
six months ago. But I didn't have some hard and fast rule about it
either. My plan was to date while pregnant, if I wanted to. Just like
my plan was to date with a baby, if I wanted to. It was my life, my
pregnancy, and my terms. So, I landed on, *Okay. Why not? I'll pick the
place.* My life, my pregnancy, my terms, and my charming, expensive Cal-Italian restaurant suggestion. We planned to meet up the
next night and neither of us pretended to be anything less than really
psyched about it.

"Maybe Ross has a roommate?" I said to Shelley, hoping that, at
thirty-six, he did not have a fucking roommate. Indifferent to any of
the above, she redirected me straight back to our manhunt.

The next night, perched at a cute trattoria that off-duty celebrities liked to hang out at, I pleasantly discovered that Ross was indeed

rugged and gorgeous, and very tall with big hands and wavy, dirty Disney Prince hair that smelled like Marlboro Reds. He drove a nice and shiny Volvo, which seemed off-brand, but I liked it. He was easy to talk to, and he thought I was hilarious, and when he told me about going to rehab, it was better than any foreplay. We shared two bowls of pasta under an outdoor terrace intertwined with wisteria, and the food and words were scrumptious and fluid, and he generously paid even though he jokingly called himself a cheap-ass bastard. Frugality aside, Ross was a lot like me. He was a really fun person. He was completely uninterested in pristine or polished; he had a hard-on for messy and real. He loved love, and took one too many chances on it, and now his heart sort of lived between frustration and fucktopia. We'd both been severely hurt more times than we could count. We had both caused other people pain, of which we either reflected on too hard, or not nearly hard enough. We were creative souls who had figured out how to make a decent living doing what we were passionate about, and that in itself felt like a secret society. We were both pathologically open people. Sophisticated *and* déclassé. Enlightened *and* inappropriate. And more than anything else, Ross and I both loved talking about sex almost as much as we loved having it.

Oh, and Ross *did* have a roommate! Ben had been Ross's best friend since childhood. They were tethered at the hip, and totally codependent. They went to the same boarding school, then Amherst College together, and they even drove nearly identical anti-hip Volvos all over East LA. We met up with Ben later that night at a chill outdoor bar in Silver Lake. Ross drank Diet Cokes like it was his job, and I learned that Ben, too, was tall, scruffy, and electromagnetic.

And single! But he was way too debaucherous for Shelley; I knew that from *Hey girl*. Whereas Ross was flawed but fundamentally grounded, Ben was darker. He had an elegant druggie vibe, a tortured trustifarian way about him. He had a big job in consulting that, he swore, was slowly killing his soul. He also had an on-again, off-again relationship that sounded as toxic as it was erotic. Be that as it may, Ben was not some bad boy cliché. He was a gem. They both were.

The three of us hung out all night long, sparing no detail about our personal lives, and it was like paradise on a picnic table. Like me, they both had easy access to their emotional baggage, and they could laugh about it and cry about it. Sure, Ross and Ben were kind of man children and shameless hos and textbook commitment phobes, but they were also astute listeners and unbelievably kind and authentically edgy. They were my kind of guys—and I don't mean that in the unshaven faces and great cocks kind of way, but because we all somehow existed on the same wavelength of happy and messy and complicated and contradictory. That kind of connectivity has always been hard for me to find, and connectivity is, after all, the eternal quest of every social being.

Ross and I kissed good night that first night, confirming the chemistry was unfortunately on fire, and I went back to New York the next morning, knowing I would be back in LA in three weeks for more meetings. From that point on, we texted a thousand times a day. Sometimes more. Our communication was manic and breathless. In less time than it took for most people to schedule a second date, Ross had become my lover and best friend. The most amazing part of it all? My impending pregnancy was never a glitch in our relationship, but a gift.

While Ross was not ready to be a father himself, and I never wavered in my conviction to do it on my own, he wholeheartedly wanted to be on this journey with me and I was more than happy to make the space for him.

Practically overnight, Ross got fully up to speed on my fertility treatment calendar. He googled Dr. Grifo. He studied Vince Vaughn's profile. He learned my cycle. If there were a MasterClass on fibroids, he would have taken it and then taught it at the David Geffen School of Medicine at UCLA. Ross knew the mornings I had to get blood work done. He knew when the vials of sperm arrived, and where they were stored and at what temperature; he reminded me about the hormone pills I had to take, and suggested that I eat pomegranates because they increase blood flow to the uterus. He FaceTimed with my mother and sister as they sat beside me at appointments, and he sent beautiful bouquets of white roses on the days of my big procedures. And when I found out I was pregnant and the baby had a heartbeat, he was the first person I called. Guess who cried harder than any of us that day. . . .

I realize all of this might sound over-the-top. Like this guy Ross had *Dexter* or *Dear John* written all over him. You're probably thinking that I make up my mind quickly, way too quickly, and often foolishly, about men—especially men who remind me of Jackson Maine in *A Star Is Born* and men who look like they build houses on the weekends and men who make you their sun around which everything orbits. But how about this theory instead: on my wondrous path toward motherhood, I was open to extraordinary things, and because of that, I met extraordinary people.

As the TV deals in LA escalated—which was also extraordinary—I started flying to LA every few weeks, and staying with Ross and Ben at their pretty Spanish-style house in the most rolling terrain of Echo Park, all lemon trees and recording studios and indie actresses with big, full bushes (Ross's preference, let it be known). When my Uber would haul itself up the steep hill that was their street and I'd see the two Volvos parked in the driveway, it was like I saw God. Ross would wait for me on their flowery porch, smoking and waving. Ben was often right beside him too, always a cherry on top, so handsome and hedonistic. They were both impossibly sweet about my pregnancy, lugging my suitcases up their mountain of a driveway, and eventually hoisting me up there too.

One night when Ross was out working in the studio, Ben and I were lounging around the living room, talking about the kind of daughter I wanted to raise. I told him I wanted her to be the kind of girl who always got up to dance at a party, because that was never me. "Oh no?" he asked, turning up the record player. *Shit*. St. Vincent was playing. "Are you sure that's not you? I think it *is* you. . . ." Before I knew it, Ben was pulling me up from the couch to rock it out together. It felt like a scene from a dream, and I couldn't help but surrender to him. Slowly, I swirled around my shoulders with my eyes closed, while he was moving and grooving, and it was such a sweet memory.

There were always so many meetings when I was in LA, and I was experiencing so much work agita, and it was an effort to keep up the stamina as I got enormously pregnant, at thirty-eight years old no less. But every night, Ross, Ben, and I would come together to eat arepas under their pergola and talk and laugh robustly as the orange-purple sun set like a Rothko painting. Together, we'd analyze all our most tender and twisted relationships, and tell, receive, and reciprocate the funniest and most fucked-up stories about love and sex. All this went on until I was too gargantuan to fly anymore and my two TV deals had to resume via conference calls.

Back in New York, to keep it simple, I called Ross my "LA Boyfriend," and I think he called me his "New York Girlfriend" too. But it was always loose and noncommittal, and we both got off on that. On weekend trips to Palm Springs and Napa Valley, we gleefully told strangers that we were a couple and that I was pregnant and that he was *not* the father. We both loved a reaction. Everything about us was outside the box. We said "I love you" the very first night we met, but we never had "the talk" in terms of defining our relationship or our rules about monogamy. In hindsight, I guess we were in an open relationship, but we never even labeled it that. We just did our thing. I didn't care who Ross was or wasn't sleeping with when I wasn't around—and I'm sure he was boning half of Los Angeles for no other reason than he could. Ross gave me an unbelievable amount of love and attention. He was literally *always* there for me. And I didn't need anything more from him than that.

Looking back, maybe I should have called Ross my "LA Lover," but we actually didn't have that much sex, as sublime as it was. As soon as I started the fertility procedures, I didn't want any confusion around the paternity of it all. Then, as I got into my second and third trimesters, I only wanted to make love to various iterations of rice, beans, cheese, guacamole, and hot sauce, anyway.

The only title I knew to be real and true was that Ross was "My Person." He was my person as I built my bridge to motherhood, and he was also my person during the drama that was selling those goddamn TV shows.

So here's how it all played out in Hollywood: After a year and a half giving these two shows everything I had—all my stories, my memories, my vulnerabilities, my pain, and every last drop of my writing prowess—the two networks attached to the projects, FOX and CBS, both passed. It was everybody's fault and nobody's fault.

The passes shouldn't have felt like such a big blow, given the odds, and yet they did. A Tina Fey series took one of the spots, and I took *some* pleasure in knowing I could even compete with her, but other than that, nothing good came of it professionally or financially. A coveted TV writer friend advised me not to disclose any sense of disappointment to anyone, as to not appear "petty." The whole thing was heartbreaking.

All the actors and producers sent sympathy texts from their glass mansions in the Hills, but I felt used, abused, and totally over it all. By the time I was ready to give birth to my daughter, I had made approximately zero dollars from TV development and had given it almost all of my time. The rejection took the professional wind out of me. The money situation was suddenly scary. I fired my agents and my lawyers—not that any of them cared, as my name had become entirely irrelevant the moment the networks passed—and I vowed to quit Hollywood for good.

Ross, on the other hand, I did not swear off like everything else in LA. As time went on, however, he naturally transitioned from boyfriend-lover-person to dear friend for life. Our romance had a reason and a season, and we both knew that, and we honored it.

Our year together made a lifelong impact on the way I would date moving forward. I had always tried to be the "cool girlfriend" in a classic, monogamous relationship structure. But even that type of setup felt too rigid after being in a relationship that was so truly free. Being with Ross taught me everything I needed to know about allowing a love story to aerate and breathe, and how to move along with it intuitively, with your own rules and expectations. Never again would I try to fit inside a traditional couple construct. Maybe I was a boring hetero, but I would always be happiest on the romantic fringe. The proof was right in front of my eyes. Of all the relationships I'd ever been in, this was the only one that combined long distance, nonmonogamy, addiction, a roommate, codependency, cigarettes, aspartame, and oh yeah, a baby from another daddy— and yet it was the healthiest and most functional relationship of my life.

While the work stuff chewed me up and spit me out, in the end, I will always feel joy thinking of Echo Park. Ross and Ben restored my heart. They were the untamed creatures I needed, when I didn't think I needed anyone at all. More than any of the other "eclectic and eccentric" people in my village, I felt the most profound acceptance and belonging with these two enchanted womanizers at their little hacienda. And what better time for such humanity than while pregnant and alone. It all made me think: *Ain't love grand?*

Which is why I'm so sorry to end on a sad note.

About two years after our special time together, tragedy struck my wonderful friends in LA. Ben died. It was an accidental drug overdose. He was forty. Ross and his new girlfriend, Amy, found him at the Echo Park house after spending a week at her place. He passed away in his bedroom, alone, and was dead for days before anyone knew. The news gutted all their friends and lovers, of which there were many, and of course, it destroyed me too. Not long after his death, Ross and Amy moved to the desert. There was no way he could stay in Echo Park, under the orange-purple sunset, without their matching Volvos in the driveway.

As Ben's life ended, my daughter's life would begin. And one day while she danced, I would tell her all about him.

thirteen

"Sex Diaries": The Column

Had you told me as a teenager that I would someday pay my bills with tales of sex parties in grocery store basements, art deco necklaces that doubled as high-wattage vibrators, and vegan lube that tasted like watermelon Jolly Ranchers, I probably would have looked at you and said, "And so?"

Hollywood left me with nothing but high blood pressure—not an insignificant detail—and a very fancy baby stroller gifted from Todd Spiewak and Jim Parsons (whom I still loved), and a bunch of selfies in front of the *Shameless* set. Weeks before giving birth to my daughter, I had no steady assignments or income coming in. My magazine work had all but dried up since I had neglected it for the TV dreams, and print journalism wasn't exactly a flourishing industry anyway. My book, *Apron Anxiety,* had gotten good reviews and had a small cult following, but a second book deal never came to fruition—not that I'd watered that garden either.

So it felt rather out of the blue when Molly Fisher, a well-liked editor at *New York* magazine whom I'd had a writer-crush on ever since she penned an essay about meeting her husband via Craigslist's "Missed Connections," emailed to see if I wanted to revive their "Sex Diaries" column and, barring any unforgivable flailings, take it over permanently.

I wasn't familiar with the column, but Molly explained that I would need to wrangle a different New Yorker each week and work with them to create a seven-day diary detailing their love and sex life. It wasn't meant to be erotica or anything like that, but we wanted an explicit look at people's relationship with intimacy. The diarists' identities would be anonymous to everyone but me, and past those parameters, I could do whatever I wanted with it.

It sounded like a fool's errand.

I appreciated that the column was a meditation on modern love and sex. That part sounded cool, and right up my alley. But how the hell would I find a different person every single week of the year to entrust me with their private bedroom stories? Wouldn't only crazy people want to participate? Plus, what a headache to edit thousands of words from blabbering sex maniacs who were not even close to professional writers.

More than anything else, though, while I was definitely in touch with my own sexuality, I was not deeply entrenched in the underbelly of sex culture. Shouldn't the column go to someone else? I wasn't queer or into kink or even inclined to much sexual exploration beyond the usual stuff. I was about to become a Basic Brooklyn Mom, after all, all Clare V. straps and rotisserie chickens and Zillow porn. In fact, after I stopped sleeping with Ross, part of me actually felt like I had experienced enough hot sex for one lifetime, and that I could now transition to other pleasures like new Real Housewife *and* Below Deck franchises. Did I really want to be inundated with stories of fucking and fighting when I could just watch it without burden on *Vanderpump Rules*?

But then another friend at *New York* magazine told me, off the record, that Molly's email wasn't entirely random. The higher-ups at *New York* heard I was about to have a baby on my own and that I was not very well funded, and they wanted to give me as much work (aka paychecks) as I was up for. The weekly "Sex Diaries" column, with its solid editorial fee, was an unspoken gift of sorts. That touched me. In Jewish tradition, it's a "mitzvah" to do something caring and generous before you're even asked to help, and furthermore, without needing or wanting any recognition for the act of kindness. This felt like a version of that, an ego-less mitzvah disguised in BJs and BDSM.

Obviously, I had to take the column. The content promised to be stimulating. I would be on the front line of love and sex in the best city in the world—what could be a more interesting beat than that? The money would sustain me. And while I had to do a bit of mental jujitsu to come around to it, it made sense that the column landed in my lap. Who better to write it than me?

My recruitment of friends and strangers with healthy sex lives was underway. My first stop was my girlfriend Ro, who, at fifty years old, still daydreams about her partner's package, all day long, even after years of co-parenting and paying the mortgage. Then I connected with my friend Riley, who believes his true calling is to be a fuckboi and has really committed to the role. I stopped random people who looked sensuous or kittenish on the street. I inserted myself into a steamy moment with a lesbian couple making out on a crosstown bus. I asked a guy in line for bagels if he was banging anybody fun. I met an NYPD officer at Starbucks whose filthy mind just oozed out of his blue uniform as he told me how much he loves cuckholding and hates being a cop. I even made Ross do a diary, where I finally fully understood just how many women regularly sit on his face. But mostly, I relied on the anonymous leads that trickled in through the "Sex Diaries" email address and often took me to new, exhilarating, and slut-positive places, most of the time in Bushwick. Bushwick makes me feel like a goddamn dinosaur.

What else would I learn as I fielded diary after diary? Obviously assplay is everything. So is punching while fucking. There are still a lot of publicists doing an obscene amount of cocaine and probably taking way too much Plan B (no judgment . . . been there). My mind was blown—which does not happen easily—by the gay male model who went to an all-night orgy that competed in "how many loads you could take." There was the super-liberal chef trying to make sense of her carnal attraction to a QAnon follower, and a scientist making love to her four-person polycule in between lab experiments. I learned about pay pigs (typically, a submissive male who gets off on financial exploitation). Unicorns (generally, a woman who joins a heterosexual couple for ongoing sex). Pillow princesses (women, usually in a queer relationship, who prefer to lie back and receive pleasure). I worked with lots of size queens, and several cougars in Connecticut. I cried for the lonely older man madly in love with his masseur, who would occasionally jerk him off and then accompany him to the cinema. Oh, and all my girls on

SeekingArrangement, getting paid for their companionship in Botox bills and Louis Vuitton bags, to which I say: *brilliant*.

All in all, it's been a privilege to edit the "Sex Diaries" column. I know it's not high art or hard work. I am not precious about it. The most challenging part has been finding people every week, and that can feel impossible at times, but the rest is cake. Sometimes I even eat cake as I work on them.

Per its original intention, "Sex Diaries" kept the lights on when I needed it most. It kept the lights on in my small one-bedroom apartment as I built my little nursery and prepared to bring a child home alone. And it still keeps the lights on now. I've had the column for over seven years (that's almost four hundred diaries!), and while I will never grow rich or famous off of it, or even graduate from the "Under Fourteen Dollars" table at the local wine shop, I am very grateful. Which is why I've never complained about the column, taken a break, or missed one single deadline.

Well, maybe just one.

A few diaries in, one month before my due date, my mom reminded me that my blood pressure was a little high at my last doctor's appointment and that I was supposed to check it daily at the local pharmacy. Because she worries, I don't have to. Therefore, I prolonged the trip to CVS, leisurely stopping for a chocolate almond croissant at a bougie bakery, then at an art shop for my friend's kid who had taken an interest in watercolors, and then to sit at Brooklyn Bridge Park for a gossip session on the phone with my good friend Hudson Morgan, whom I worked with on developing the *See Alyssa Date* show.

Hud is the best conversationalist in the world, but it was hard to focus on anything he had to say with my mother texting every two minutes hawking me to "check the BP."

"Lemme call you right back, Huddles," I said to him, dragging myself to the pharmacy section of a CVS down the street.

When I finally put my arm in the blood pressure sleeve and saw that the numbers were high, I obviously blamed it on Hud and me talking about Hollywood dramz, and nothing more than that.

When the numbers were even higher at the Walgreens I walked over to next, and then off the charts at a big Duane Reade, I had no choice but to call my obstetrician and read her all the results from the last three screenings. I nonchalantly gave her the figures, and she immediately told me to get in a taxi and come straight to the hospital.

"To your office?"

"To the eighth floor, Labor and Delivery," she responded imperatively.

"Ohhhh. Shit. Like, go to the hospital 'with my bag' *go to the hospital*? Wait, I'm not really packed. How many pairs of pajamas do you think . . . ?"

"Alyssa, get here right away. Okay?"

This was not about Hollywood-related stress, though it certainly was a plot twist. It was preeclampsia. I was about to have a stroke.

Thankfully, I got to NYU Langone just in time. Moments before the nurses wheeled me into the operating room for an emergency C-section, lovingly and nervously surrounded by my mother, father, and sister, who had rushed there with me, I asked for my iPhone.

Typing as fast as I could, while the gurney was literally being pushed out the door, I fired off an email to my "Sex Diaries" editor that week.

I had been a professional writer almost my entire life, since I was a fourteen-year-old staff member of the *Springfield Union News*. But this was the first and only time I tried my hand at . . . poetry.

Hey there. The diary might be a few days late. I'm having a baby tonight.

fourteen

Transcendence

Dr. Margaret Durante, whom I had never heard of or met before, was on call the night I was rushed to the hospital. She was about my age, with a compassionate disposition, a quiet empowerment, and a great freckled face resembling an Ivy League Emma Stone. When Dr. Durante learned that I did not have a partner, was a Single Mom by Choice, and that the handsome older gentleman who was accompanying me to the OR was my father, I could almost see inside her head as she paused her whip-smart OB-GYN brain to set a softer intention, which was to give me all her love.

She warmly suggested I call her Meg, which I did.

In the movies, getting stuck in the delivery room with a new doctor who doesn't know anything about your background or your body or even your blood type causes some women to catastrophize. And justifiably so. But for some unknowable reason, I was overcome with a more karmic outlook the night I almost stroked out and had an emergency C-section: Meg was meant to keep me alive and deliver my daughter in good health. Simply because I felt a strong affinity for her, I had absolute confidence that she was the right person to do both of those things. In fact, I found myself in a totally illogical state of blind, existential faith, assured that everything was the way it was meant to be that night. Despite the fact that I was extremely sick, four weeks early, unpartnered, on an operating table, and unprepared for *any* of this—let's pause to take in the enormity of that—I was very much okay.

"So, yeah, Dr. Grifo actually got me pregnant. Do you know him?" I asked Meg while lying under the most unflattering fluorescent surgical lights, as she carefully prepared for the C-section. My dad was sitting right behind me, but he knew enough to give us some uninterrupted time and space to get comfortable with each other.

"He froze my eggs!" she said, looking up cheerfully, which automatically transformed what might have felt like an impending autopsy into a bottomless champagne brunch.

"Don't you fucking love him?" I squealed, suddenly embarrassed to have sworn in front of my elegant doctor and her team of bright young things.

Though Meg was careful not to cross any professional lines, she confirmed that most women shared my sentiments on Grifo. (I told her I wouldn't trust someone who didn't!) And as we connected on our dreamboat fertility doctor, she simultaneously continued to focus on, you know, the upcoming task of slicing me open and pulling out a tiny human from my loins.

Given that she was about to know everything and then some about my uterus and stomach and pelvis and bladder, I took it a little further. "Do you have a partner, Doctor?" I wasn't sure what her deal was. *Married? Single? Poly? LGBTQ+?*

Before she could answer, the anesthesiologist entered the room. He wore tie-dye scrubs and a seventies bandanna and seemed like the type of vegetarian who chain-smoked cigarettes, or the sketchy kind of Burning Man man, and I wasn't so sure about him. As someone gently bent me forward and untied my gown in the back, the Burner began to administer an epidural into my spine. It took a while to get it right (which I heard happens sometimes), and it was not exactly a spa treatment, though I tried to downplay the discomfort of being stabbed in the spinal cord by a doctor whose vibrations I wasn't so sure about.

Meg distracted me from the several epidural do-overs by jumping in with the good stuff. Yes, she had a boyfriend. It was new. He was a waiter she'd met on vacation with her girlfriends. He was French and lived on an island! They had some kinks to iron out, starting with the long distance, but she believed he was a genuinely good man, and she felt lucky he came into her life.

The epidural was done.

As the drugs kicked in, one of the nurses told me her lover was transitioning. Someone else said her latest date wanted to lick her hair. And another nurse said it seemed like everyone online was now ethically nonmonogamous. Now. Was I about to be cut in half with a couple key organs removed from my body and then put back in, hopefully where they belonged? Yup. Was this dangerous pre-eclampsia bullshit going to try to kill me again, after the baby was

out? Probably so. Did I really need to continue this juicy and ther-
apeutic girl talk with my new obstetrician and everyone else in the
surgery room? Yes. Yes, I did.

"Your romance with the waiter is such a screenplay," I cooed to
Meg as they all made the final preparations for the Cesarean section. I told her that when all this was over, she at least had to do a
Sex Diary for me. She laughed that off, joking—even though it was
true—that she was a good Catholic girl.

"Fair enough," I said, silently relieved that she, too, was saying
her prayers.

The medical team put up a drape from my waist down and began
conversing in doctortalk that went way above my head. All I knew
was they were ready to operate.

"Meg?" I interrupted, just before go time, slurring a little. The
drugs were working. I was numb from my neck down. "Do you
think you could love him forever?"

"You know what, Alys? I do. I really do," she said wistfully, with
the genuine sweetness and hope that, I swear, set the tone for my
baby's entrance into the world, if not for her eternal being.

"So don't let him go," I said, resigned *not* to the fact that I did not
have a forever love myself but to the fact that surgery was about to
begin and it was time for me to shut the fuck up.

Then, like clockwork, just before the first incision, one of the
nurses said, "Has anyone ever told you you're just like Carrie Bradshaw?!"

By now, my mind and body were in a really woozy state, and I was
disengaging from reality, but I managed to smile and mean it and nod
with amusement. "Mmhmmmm," I hummed, closing my eyes.

It was time to get serious. No more talking. I told my dad that I was going to disappear from all this and to please not break my trance. "Just know, Daddy, I'm not dead. I'm just drifting away." As Meg began to cut, my dad sat behind me, gently rubbing my shoulders, and I tried to remember the meditation from Switzerland. The one we'd said in the snow. But I couldn't remember the words. So I meditated in a new way that I had no idea I was capable of. I detached from my body completely and landed somewhere in the Caribbean with soft taupe sand and bright turquoise water. It was the ultimate exercise in calmness and stillness, and again, though the spiritual way was not what I planned or prepared for, it was my life raft that night.

Every few minutes, however, I would deliberately break from the beach and take inventory of things. The journalist in me sought some texture and color, I guess. After all, there I was, a witness to human creation, a once-in-a-lifetime thing. What do I remember? Well, this is very trite, but the dominating thought was how parched I was! All I wanted was a Diet Sprite, which was so specific, considering I'm not much of a soda drinker. I also remember asking someone whose hands were not inside my body to please tell my mother and sister that I was doing just fine. (I asked them to do this every few minutes actually.) I remember the extreme love I felt for Meg and her staff, and expressing my overwhelming gratitude for them, over and over until there I was, being a blabbermouth again. But the most remarkable memory I can carve out from the emergency C-section is this: Though I was undergoing major abdominal surgery and subconsciously traumatized by the preeclampsia and only moments away from the emotional earthquake that was new motherhood, I can say without a doubt that there was not one second of childbirth that I wished for a husband to be standing there beside me. The thought never even crossed my mind.

My daughter, Hazel Delilah Shelasky, came into the world at 9:58 that night. She was just under six pounds—small, but not quite a preemie, and definitely mighty. As Meg lifted her from my womb into the arms of my father, the only words I could say were "Is she healthy? Is she healthy? Is she healthy?" And she was. Then someone put some ice cubes in my mouth, and my eyes rolled to the back of my head from the sweet relief of the hydration. My tearful dad gently placed Hazel on my body. I was so numb and drugged by then that I couldn't get my face muscles to smile, even though it was the greatest moment of my life. It wasn't until I puked up the Percocet that I could actually express just how wonderful she was.

In the blink of an eye, my mother and sister were back by my side, and my baby and I were in the recovery room. There was so much excitement and celebration. So many texts and emails and homemade soups and bouquets of sunflowers, just from my best friends alone. I was so fortunate to be so supported as a single mom that all I could wish for was for every other single mom in the world to feel this level of care. But I was also physically and emotionally weak—weaker than I ever imagined I would or could be—so I sent everyone home around midnight, knowing they'd be back in the morning. *Mama needs a minute.*

Throughout the night, the amazing nurses came in and out to check on my blood pressure (which was not good, but with more heavy drugs, we got a handle on it) and to help me with breastfeeding when they could. In hindsight, maybe it would have been a little easier if I had a partner beside me, to lift the baby from her adjoining crib to my bandaged body every time she cried, as I could not move, or sit up on my own, not with my stomach just barely stitched back together again. But I figured things out by myself. Like everything else to come, Hazel and I would find the systems that worked for us.

As it were, everyone from the hospital gushed over Hazel's beauty, which was—my goodness—breathtaking. Her skin was like buttercream, her lips were rosebuds, and she had the most unbelievably iconic eyebrows for a baby who was literally one day old. One nurse said she looked like Nicole Kidman; another nurse said Cate Blanchett.

When I looked at the baby, I saw myself and my family, now and generations before. I saw the picture of the donor that I'd gazed at hundreds of times. I saw Dr. Grifo. I saw Meg. I saw Ross. And Ben. I saw all my close friends, who were waiting with bated breath with *Goodnight Moon*s and Sophie la Girafes. I saw Rome. I saw Chelsea Piers and my shaking legs running away from normal. I saw my book, and my columns, and all my failures, and all my wins. I saw God and I saw heaven. But mostly, I saw my little fig, my daughter, my child, my Hazy.

fifteen

One Foot in Front of the Other

L ila Cohen had a private room at the other end of the maternity ward.

She was a beautiful, bubbly foodie influencer, aka a "foodlebrity." She was also known to be smart, philanthropic, and fiercely pro-women, and everyone I knew from the New York City media world said she was "really good people."

Lila had a baby boy at NYU the same night as me, just a few operating rooms away, and although we had never met before, all our mutual friends believed it to be kismet that we'd experienced the magic of childbirth just a few nurse stations and one vending machine away from each other.

Lila Cohen is somewhere on your floor, go say hi!! texted my friend Brooke. *Tell me what you think of her hot Israeli husband....* DMed my friend Julie. *I had Breads Bakery send Lila a babka; you should swing by and have some!* emailed my friend Danielle Praport. None of the above enticed me in the least. *Eh,* I thought, *I don't need any new friends. What I* need *are new nipple protectors.* Hazel was nursing nonstop.

Snarkily, I did wonder: *What did Lila name the kid?* Almond? Roux? Manchego? The hypocrisy that I myself had published a food memoir with recipes and written years of clickbait on topics like the religion of ranch dressing and "Rainy Day Rigatoni" didn't occur to me at the time. All I knew was that I was not up for designer doughnuts with a rich, skinny, pretty person who was probably posting pictures of some whack placenta pie.

Even my sister, Rachel—who has very good judgment barring the two consecutive years she zealously auditioned for *The Bachelor*—liked this Lila Cohen woman. They had been out to dinner together before. And my sister is a genuinely nice person, who likes genuinely nice people. So three days postpartum, when Rach gently suggested I try to walk for the first time since my Cesarean section and use Lila's room as an end goal, I said, this time out loud, "I Do Not Need New Friends. Dr. Durante filled the last spot. Friend shop closed."

Okay. So . . . did I become a mother and instantly turn into a motherfucker? No. But something was going on. A storm was brewing. Health-wise, I was in rough shape. When you have preeclampsia, you're put on a magnesium drip to prevent seizures, which makes you feel at first like you're on heroin and then like you're coming off heroin. I was in the ugliest withdrawal stage of the drug, and I couldn't shake the nausea. Much of my midsection was still caked in blood. There was a catheter inside my urethra, and if we're zeroing in on private parts, I smelled like ass. Because I kept vomiting up the painkillers and was adamant about not taking any more, I was also in unrelenting pain from head to toe. I hadn't slept in at least seventy-two hours—I was so tired that when I did finally have the energy to reach for my iPhone, the first thing I typed was "Can you die from no sleep?" Plus, this was day three in the hospital and because my blood pressure would not stabilize, they were not letting me out anytime soon, which frustrated me beyond words. So there was all that.

However, I did have to try to walk before my legs began to atrophy. Doctor's orders. Hazel was asleep in the room, and my father was there to watch over her, so this was indeed the time. With another aggressive push from my sister, I reluctantly said we could make our way toward the big LC. But first I had to try to stand up. I took a deep breath that begged for mouthwash, and my mother helped me slowly rise from the bed. It felt utterly debasing to be so shaky and needy in front of people, even my own people, but there was no other way to do this. As I found my footing and balanced my legs, we carefully, slowly, started to move me out the door. One foot in front of the other.

It was nothing short of brutal walking down the long and drab hospital corridor, with my mother and sister holding me up, still hooked to tubes and properly dope sick, but at some point, I found myself at Lila Cohen's door. We didn't even need to know the room number. All we had to do was follow the uproarious sounds of laughter and festivity and joking and noshing and kvelling and . . . *knock, knock.*

The three of us stood at the entrance to Lila's suite, and before anyone noticed us, I took in the atmosphere with my hollowed-out eyes. She had her distinguished-looking parents there, along with her equally upscale in-laws. Lots of Prada Sport. Lots of Crème de la Mer moisturizer. They were all surrounded by trays of delicious treats to be eaten over *L'chaims* and nostalgia. Her handsome husband was fixing Lila a plate or a schmear, while telling some adorable and embarrassing story, which was, of course, all about her. There was a palpable sense of unity and closeness. Not to mention, Lila's hair was bouncy and brushed, and she had just enough makeup on to look camera-ready but not like a Kardashian. I even liked her athleisurewear—in all its Instagrammability. *Why am I still in my ragged hospital gown? Is it even tied in the right places?* We quickly overheard that Lila's son's name was not Arugula but Grayson, which is a great name, and they were all planning out Grayson's bris, which sounded special and lovely. The whole scene was special and lovely and the fact of the matter was: it was just too hard for me to see.

As my sister finally introduced us from the doorway, Lila and her family waved us in warmly. But I could not proceed with any of it. Instead I turned my head from them, and twisted my broken body around, and said to no one, and not particularly discreetly, "Get me the hell out of here." I was about to cry. The dam was about to break. Everyone could see it. My mother quickly maneuvered me away. Lila Cohen was not someone I was comfortable crying in front of. Frankly, I don't even like to cry in front of my own family. All I wanted to do was get back to my room and sob by myself. My only hope was to hold the tears back long enough to get there. "Let's go!" I snapped.

Once we were in the clear, it only got worse.

Because outside Lila's room, my mother said what felt like the cruelest thing anyone has ever said to me.

"Oh, come on, Alyssa. I thought you were stronger than this."

Everything devolved from there. The tears began to stream. How dare she weaponize my vulnerability. The most polite words I could bring myself to say were: "FUCK OFF and give me some privacy!"

Back in bed, I was hysterical and inconsolable and I didn't know why, but I did know that I had to cry with abandon. Furthermore, I knew I was entitled to as much time and space as I needed for that to happen. This was my room and my body and my blistering anger, and I wanted to be by myself! So after quickly and clumsily helping Hazel back onto my breast, because I still couldn't physically do that myself, the Shelasky crew bolted to the cafeteria. They looked incredibly worried about me, which pissed me off even more. "Stop fucking judging me!" I hollered as they all scurried off like mice.

After that, heavy tears gushed for several hours. I cried so hard and for so long that a "pain management" doctor came to my room and asked if I needed a sedative, or maybe it was a tranquilizer. Not only did I tell him to "FUCK OFF and give me some privacy" too, but I threatened to report him if he ever came back to push more drugs on me again. "Ever hear of the opioid fucking crisis?" I wailed after he ran off. "Take it easy with your pill-pushing, bro!"

When my sister gently knocked on my hospital room door later that afternoon, cracking it open just enough to trepidatiously tell me she brought me a La Colombe iced latte (historically, my cure for everything), I roared that if she knocked one more time, "I would *never*—"

A terrified Rach shut the door before I could finish the threat. "But leave the *fucking* coffee!" I screamed. She re-cracked open the door, booked the iced latte over to my side table, gave Hazel the quickest kiss, and sped right back out.

Moments later, my sweet brother-in-law, Adam, stopped by with a gorgeous bouquet of flowers, and I could not so much as say *thank you*. He read the room, made it quick, and managed to safely escape.

Was this repugnant behavior on my part? Yes. I take full ownership of that. But it was like there was a demon inside me that day—and though I knew nothing about anything in terms of postpartum mental health, I knew I had to release it. I have never been so inexplicably enraged and unhinged in my entire life, and although I honor and embrace the notion that we are different after giving birth, this was way beyond my grasp of myself.

Then Ross called. He had checked in with me every few hours since Hazel was born. In between my howling, I told him that things had gone awry. That the tears would not stop, and I was one raw nerve, and possibly having a psychotic break, or maybe I just needed a good seven-hour cry or at least one hour of sleep. Hell if I knew what was happening. Between sniffles and sobs, I vowed that none of this meant that I didn't love Hazel or motherhood because I promised—I *promised*—I did. "I know, honey," he said lovingly. "I know."

I put my phone on speaker and placed it on my lap. Without words, without explaining myself, and without apology, I wailed for about ninety more minutes while he listened quietly. As I finished off my tears and waited for the clouds to break, he stayed with me however he could.

And then I felt better. The exorcism was complete.

Night had fallen. My family had gone back to Brooklyn. The doctors had switched shifts. Lila Cohen was discharged from NYU and getting to know her Tibetan night nurse at home over a hot bowl of New York's most coveted chicken soup, or so I imagined. Hazel, who had my back through all of this, was sleeping skin to skin against my bare chest, her warm, little baby heartbeat against mine. She was so refined.

Retrospectively, I now understand that my harrowing meltdown was largely due to the hormones. Hormones on hormones on hormones, and sleep deprivation, and drug withdrawal, and hormones. Chemically speaking, day three postpartum brain is typically vicious. Some midwives and doulas prepare their new moms for that, but no one told me it was normal, not that anything could have tempered the immense powerlessness I felt over my emotions that afternoon. Luckily for me, the agony stopped there, but I will never judge or dismiss, or *especially* try to defuse, a woman struggling with postpartum depression or anything adjacent after experiencing such wicked despair at a time when all eyes are on you, and everyone expects only sunshine and bliss.

Beyond the hormones, I've since had time to reflect on the meltdown a little more. And what I've come to unearth is heavy, and hard to admit, but I think ultimately healthy as far as self-awareness goes.

The Lila Cohen incident was a Sliding Door Moment of my life. If you don't know what that means, it's from the Gwyneth Paltrow movie *Sliding Doors,* about how one decision can change your life forever. How one move will put you on a completely different path from the one on which you were headed, posing the existential question: What would my life look like in an alternate universe?

Lila had chosen the exact life I'd walked away from so many years ago. She married a nice guy, *a real winner*. He was handsome and family-oriented, and would provide for her, dote on her, schmear for her. Lila's life seemed stable and comfortable; they owned a three-bedroom apartment; they had well-vetted "staff." She would send yearly holiday cards with Grayson wearing Janie and Jack, and have epic kid birthday parties with six-layer rainbow cakes baked by Christina Tosi herself. The entrance of their home would have a doormat that read *Oh, Hello!* in cursive, and an entire wall of black-and-white family photos would be framed beautifully via Framebridge. On weekends they would apple-pick while casually browsing houses in Chappaqua, only to return to the city reinvigorated by their proximity to things like Singaporean street food, and so much culture! Lila and her hubby would take luxurious, kid-free vacations to Los Cabos and Lisbon and have scheduled Saturday night sex throughout the year, which she would engage in only to keep her marriage healthy, and it would *all* be good enough for both of them—forever.

Lila Cohen's hospital room was a glimpse into what my hospital room would have looked like had I stayed on a more traditional track, had I played it safer, had I done things the right way. And the whole scene was a trigger. Because the truth was . . . her world . . . her little ecosystem? It did not look so bad. It was not unimaginative or one-dimensional or dreadful in any way. Her life seemed filled with happiness. And I found that to be absolutely heartbreaking.

Because by comparison, it left me with a sinking suspicion that my life was very much *other*. Sure, I chose *other*. I chose unconventionality. And I still didn't wish to have a husband; I still cherished my freedom and independence. But alone in a room with an oozing stomach wound, unconventionality is not Hemingway or Bon Iver or jagged bangs or *Just Kids*. It's just lonely. My cool little life didn't feel so radical at the hospital. It felt radically . . . alienating. I knew I was just tired, and the hormones were bigger than me, and the drugs were messing with my brain chemistry, but in the dark silence of the night, as I sang off-key lullabies and Jewish hymns to Hazel, praying I'd be healthy enough to go home soon, I felt stranded and abandoned by my very own self.

A few years later I saw Lila Cohen at a friend's baby shower. She looked great as always, and to say the least, I was in much better shape than the last time we'd crossed paths. We exchanged pictures of Grayson and Hazel, and bonded over the life-changing date of October 3, 2015.

We caught up a little. Lila was having a tough time with secondary infertility. She could get pregnant, but she kept miscarrying, which meant she had lost multiple babies, and some of them late-term. She and her husband had been through rounds and rounds of IVF, as well as one adoption that fell through at the last minute. It was taking a toll on her marriage and her body. I felt so sad to hear she had been through so much suffering.

"I have to apologize if I wasn't so nice in the hospital," I said, after a few anxious gulps of sparkling water. "Your life just looked so amazing, and . . ." She nearly spit out her mimosa at "amazing."

We laughed a little, and then I continued. "It just made me wonder if I made the wrong choices . . . if I cheated myself of a better future outcome. In hindsight, I was just having a moment, and obviously I wouldn't change a thing, because then I wouldn't have Hazel. But I think I resented you for awakening those feelings within me. And I just wanted to be honest about that."

Lila said all she remembered was how uniquely close me and my family were, and how comforted she was to have a friendly face nearby. She might have been letting me off the hook, or maybe that's how she registered our brief encounter, but either way I appreciated the words.

At the end of our catch-up, Lila gave me a big hug, and as I wrapped my arms around her body, I hoped only the best things for my friend, who, of course, I had plenty of room for in my life.

We kissed each other on the cheek. Then we both snuck off to call our kids.

sixteen

Mommy & Not Me

I had no business whatsoever joining a mommy & me group. It was never going to end well.

But the truth was, I absolutely loved being a new mom. Hazel and I found our groove pretty quickly, and I thought, what better way to display our high-functioning capabilities than to join a group of ladies with Oeuf cribs and Monstera plants and babies all named Annabelle to bond about it?

Life with a nocturnal newborn wasn't easy by any means, but I had dreamed about the sheer exhaustion and raw nipples and gross diapers and general overwhelm for so long that I felt ongoingly stupefied to be so "in it." Life with a baby was so much happier than life *without* a baby and as long as I could pause and remind myself of that, I felt good.

After about a week back home, I even went halfway "back to work," filing my columns and drafting book proposals, now about "parenting" naturally. Surprisingly, more than one publisher told me that the marketplace had "motherhood fatigue," which seemed kind of crazy considering *we make all the people,* but I went back to love and sex with a greater appreciation for my flexible career than ever. (Keep in mind, unlike 99.9 percent of working moms in this country, work for me meant puttering around in my Anthropologie bathrobe and then typing on the keyboard whenever the caffeine hit my bloodstream, and if it did not hit my bloodstream, I'd just watch *Friday Night Lights,* and tell myself that tomorrow was a new day. You can't compare my situation as a single working mom to most.)

Whether there's any merit to this or not, I also believed that my partnerlessness was an asset during those first few months. With just my baby and myself, there was a lot less to manage than if I had to juggle a marriage, too. My autonomy never felt more useful than during those first few weeks of my daughter's life. If I wanted to assemble a chocolate-chia-banana smoothie while simultaneously breastfeeding, or lie in Savasana on the rug for the entire day, or lumber around all night long naked and sweaty and fleshy, then, *cool.* If I wanted to eat cold pad Thai for breakfast and Trader Joe's Scandinavian Swimmers for dinner, who was looking? If my one-month-old daughter's only social interaction was with *The Real Housewives of Atlanta, Beverly Hills,* and *NewYork,* I considered all of them our crazy aunties, and saw nothing wrong with spending so much time together.

So why not throw a mom group into the mix? This could be fun, I thought, filling out my credit card information for ten Tuesday morning sessions. And *that's* when things went a little—as Hazel would eventually say as a toddler—*wonky donky.*

The group of eight moms, along with their babies, met at a kids' play center within walking distance from my apartment, in a small, colorful space in Cobble Hill that reminded me of a cheerful visiting room inside a mental institution. The aesthetics were very: "Keep Calm & Mommy On."

As we checked in and said our hellos, I quickly learned that the leader, who was a professional social worker, took our cohort very seriously. I think she saw the gathering more like immersive group therapy of which she was the authority figure, rather than a cute group playdate for boobs-out and zonked-out creative-minded Brooklyn moms who came to laugh at themselves, engage in some low-key camaraderie, and maybe snag a free LaCroix (which is what I thought I'd signed up for).

Had I known it would be such an intense—and frankly humorless—program, I might have chosen another type of baby hang. The kind with "mom juice," as these ladies might call it. But I had paid in advance, so there I was, sitting crisscross applesauce in a circle, doing as told. As the new moms nursed their babies or rocked them in their swaddles or let them stretch out on the cushioned floor, we were told to take a deep breath and set an intention. That's when I secretly began to craft an exit strategy. My intention was to get the fuck out. Next up, we had to go around the room and share our highs and lows of the week. *Uch, really?*

Save me, my eyes said as I looked around the room for some sisterhood and solidarity. But the moms were practically bursting at the seams to unload. *All right, good for them,* I thought, *but I'm not in the mood.* Hazel, all eyebrows and baby hiccups, happily played with some wooden blocks by my lap, while I figured out how to make myself scarce.

Unless I made a scene, which I simply didn't have the energy to do, there was no way out. Fortunately, I would be the one to talk last, as I had no idea what to say and needed some time to write a soliloquy for myself. For someone who's made a career out of navel-gazing, I hadn't spent too much time checking in with myself since becoming a mom. I was fundamentally happy, and that was all I needed to know. After so many years of wondering and worrying if I'd be okay, I finally was okay. More than okay. And I wanted to sit there for a minute; I deserved to sit there for a minute. Unfortunately, the MSW wasn't going to let me. So, I had to come up with some realness and stat. But first, I listened to the others.

Mom number one—who wore a designer romper that I know for a fact cost $600 (no judgment) and was hydrating from a water bottle that read *WIFEY* (judgment)—said her low was about struggling with her husband's mother, who was too controlling and an undercover lush. Her high, on the flip side, was that her husband's bonus had come in, and it meant they could finally start shopping for weekend homes out east. "I have a great broker in Amagansett," one of the moms nudged.

The second woman was worried her live-in nanny had a closer connection to the baby than she did, but then again, she and her husband had started making love again. I think she was the first sexual being in the world whom I didn't care to recruit for a Sex Diary.

The third woman was an absolute sourpuss, which I very much appreciated, and thought I could maybe like her. She lamented that she was constantly fighting with her lawyer husband, who wasn't helping much because he had workaholic tendencies. When he tried to redeem himself with a spa overnight (her "high," obviously), it was all ruined when she forgot to pack her breast pump, prompting the husband to angrily drive it to Connecticut . . . and . . . yeah, are you snoring yet? Because I was.

Listen, I enjoy a champagne problem. But champagne problems without any self-awareness? Boring. And kill me.

As I listened to the other new moms, I kept experiencing the strangest sensation: at once I felt like I was both better than everyone *and* completely inferior to them. And maybe it was because of that fragmented feeling that I decidedly did not want to speak when it was my turn.

"Can I pass?" I asked earnestly, without affectation. I mean, where would I even begin? It felt too exhausting on top of the exhaustion to unpack my whole life story to all the married ladies. And while I wasn't trying to hide it, I didn't want to be reduced to the token alternative parent, the girl who made the group feel more inclusive.

Let me just say, these were all nice enough women—a few of whom I could almost guarantee would pull me aside after the session to say that they, too, identified as single moms, because their husbands were ALWAYS traveling for work! (Just, nooooo.) Which is all to say, our lives were not the same, our struggles were not the same, and point-blank I did not want to connect with them. I wished only good things for the seven random wifeys, but they were not going to enrich the soil for me, and I did not belong there. Every mother deserves a safe space to be seen and heard, but every mother also deserves the agency to say, *Nope, no thank you, not interested.*

The leader, whom I was now officially terrified of, wouldn't let me off the hook so easily. She said I had to say something. Anything. "You got this," she insisted with "tough love" that made me hate her.

"Well, I don't have a husband," I began slowly, swallowing the little lump in my throat that had somehow snuck up on me. "So . . . my experience is really different from all of yours."

Silence.

"Anyway, I guess my low is . . . no offense . . . but right now? Because, well, it's not your fault, but I don't think I belong here and I don't really want to be in this room anymore."

The new moms looked offended. That made me feel guilty. They hadn't done anything wrong. I mean, I'm sure they all bought those candles that smelled like Gwyneth Paltrow's vagina, but I could potentially get behind that.

"And your high?" asked the leader, really crackin' the vulnerability whip.

"Um, maybe being here is *also* my high?" I had to land the plane somewhere. "Because this feels new and hard, and yet I'm getting through it, and I think maybe that's what motherhood is all about?"

That'll do her.

"Look," I said, "having a baby on my own was the best decision of my life and the joy of that far outweighs any of my hardships, or 'lows,' so I don't really think about the darker stuff. If anything, motherhood has been a very purifying experience for me. I know that's not what you're looking for, but it's all I got. I hope you can all respect that."

Reader, by now you know I can be a bit of a bitch.

But that was not my intention here. That was truly my point of view. I was finally a mom. It was difficult to make that happen. It took a lot of self-acceptance and all sorts of strength. Yet here we were, Mama and Hazy, and it was glorious. I'm not saying I was happier than the other women. It helped having no one to be mad at all the time. It also helped that I was not a perfectionist—in fact I am whatever the opposite of a perfectionist is—which meant that I never worried about falling short, or upholding some weird standard of supermom. At the end of the day, it just seemed like my life with Hazel was more *free of suffering*—simply because I designed it that way. As far as I was concerned, we were truly all good.

If anything, my microdramas as a single mom were mostly logistical, and I wasn't going to bore anyone with that. It was murderous to get up and down the subway steps alone, lifting and carrying a clunky, heavy baby stroller, which contained a tiny, fragile baby, who could always fall right out of the carriage and into the rat-filled train tracks. Sometimes strangers were super-helpful; other times everyone pretended to be on their phone. Ubers and taxis were too expensive and who would help me install the hyper-complicated car seat anyway? Someone from NASA? Airport travel, alone with a kid, was a whole new level of torture, and yet, I kept doing it. When Hazel was a few months old, I took a few TV meetings in LA. Navigating JFK with a fussy baby, a huge suitcase, an overflowing diaper bag, a gargantuan stroller, and a giant car seat would give a Buddhist monk a nervous breakdown. In line for one flight, when someone angrily accused me of stepping on her toe, I flew into a fit of indignation, violently screaming that she was lucky that's all I did to her! And then security came. Fortunately, security was a single mom.

Hazel and I never went to another mommy & me again.

Because soon enough, we got very busy being us. We would weave and bob around Brooklyn every day, all day, eating breakfast burritos on the waterfront while listening to Ella Jenkins and Adele. With Hazel wrapped around my body in a BabyBjörn, I brought her to every press event, press trip, pitch meeting, and book brainstorm. We threw epic dinner parties for all my friends, moms or not, and in nourishing them, we nourished ourselves. Hazel never once slept in her crib, not for some attachment parenting theory (not that I knew what that meant) but because we loved being close while we dreamed. Everywhere we went there were little fireworks. We were exhausted, but our enjoyment of life together was inexhaustible.

Our mommy & me group was Alyssa & Hazel Shelasky. We belonged only to each other. And we were just beginning.

seventeen

The Powerful Man

Both of our babies had sopping wet diapers when I told my sister we had to leave LA immediately.

"You take the kids, I'll pack," I said, rushing past a tray of chocolate-covered strawberries, frantically throwing Hazel's little beach tunics into our suitcase. Rachel did not yet know what had happened down Sunset Boulevard at the fancier hotel where I went to "interview" the powerful man, but she knew it was bad. My little sister had never seen me so scared.

"Lys, what happened? Are you okay? Why are you crying?"

"I'm fine. I'll tell you everything when we're out of here. Just put the kids in the double stroller and go. I'll meet you outside."

"Where are we going?" she asked, now panicked. Our flights back to New York weren't for another few days, and we were already in over our heads with the fussy babies and no extra help. This was supposed to be a relaxing sisters' getaway—a West Coast assignment I parlayed into a little vacay in honor of our new lives as mamas and aunties. What was meant to be a week of club sandwiches by the pool and babies' first splash in the ocean, plus a half day of work for me, had turned into a nightmare I never could have imagined.

"Promise, I'll figure it all out, but we gotta leave now."

After my sister scooped up Charlie, who was just over one year old, and Hazel, who was still an infant, and left the room, I collected myself just enough to call the powerful man's publicist, who worked somewhere in West Hollywood. I had never met her before in person, but judging by her Instagram, she seemed like the kind of woman who would wear every iteration of a cashmere sweater that read *Women Rule the World*.

As she started to rave about the powerful man's latest projects and all the plugs, philanthropy, and talking points she hoped I'd include in my future story, I quickly cut her off.

"Listen. Your client just sexually assaulted me. As you know, we were supposed to meet in the lobby of the hotel, but he texted me to meet in some suite instead. He said 'everyone' was up there, which I assumed meant you and the rest of his team, and when I seemed hesitant, he added that the cabana had been converted into a pressroom. Maybe I shouldn't have fallen for it, but I did. I mean, he's not known to be some . . . I never thought of him as a . . ." My voice broke. I felt sick and dizzy, but I pushed myself to get the whole story out.

"Anyway. When I got there, it took me a minute to realize he was alone. He quickly locked the door behind us. When I tried to extract myself from the situation, he kept coming closer and closer to me. He tried to kiss me, first against the couch and then against the door that I was trying to leave from. I said 'No!' again and again, but then he thrusted the erection under his sweatpants onto me, while paw-ing at my face, moaning, 'You know you want it.' And then I finally pushed him away and ran out of there."

In retelling the event carefully, with precision, without any ten-tativeness, I felt slightly more functional, but my entire body was still rocking back and forth. As I waited for her response, my heart was beating so fast, I thought I might have a heart attack. This was about a year and a half before the Me Too movement took off, and as such, I had absolutely no idea or example of what should, or should not, happen next.

"Oh my," the publicist said, in a colder tone than I was anticipat-ing or comfortable with. "We've never had any problems like that before. He's happily married. They have a new baby. I just can't see him doing that. . . ."

"Well, he did," I declared, leaving no room for debate.

Either the publicist didn't know what to say—and I suppose that's understandable—or she was making quick calculations on how to resolve this "PR nightmare" and that gave her pause, but her response was not one of empathic concern. And the message was received: she was not an ally. I assured her that I had no interest in being a PR nightmare, and that I simply—perhaps, incorrectly—assumed she would want to know what had happened.

"Look, I'm not going to write a piece about it," I said, now con-soling *her*. "You don't have to worry. I just thought you might want to know the details because I obviously won't be profiling him in *any* magazine, and I'm going to leave LA immediately because I don't feel safe here, especially with my young daughter around. But much more important than any of that is this: You can never send a journalist to meet with this man alone again. Promise me, you will never do that. . . ."

Dead air.

I felt like I might pass out.

"Are you even there?" I had to ask.

"Alyssa, I'm just speechless. This is not the man I know."

Our call was going nowhere. She either didn't believe me, or she was in total crisis-management mode since this was a client who paid a hefty retainer. But regardless, this woman was not processing the information in a way that felt right to me, and I had no time for it. She offered to send us all to dinner, at any restaurant of our choice, to which I grimly said, "Sure." And then we hung up. I needed to feed everyone while I searched for new flights anyway.

Cut to: a random Airbnb somewhere near LAX. I couldn't find an affordable flight until the next day, but at least we were in an undisclosed location. I know that sounds paranoid, but I guess that's how terror works. The rental smelled like Parliament Lights and all the furniture was made of white pleather, and I don't remember exactly what it cost per night or if it came with Pack 'n Plays, but it was there that I could start to reinhabit my body and tell my sister what had transpired in the hotel suite.

Though there is no one easier to talk to than Rachel, it embarrassed me to unload everything onto her. I'm the older, and technically more bulletproof, sister. How did this happen to me? The whole scene was so gross and unoriginal. A man in a position of power lured me to a sketchy room. He touched me inappropriately and nonconsensually. He even said, "You know you want it." It was like a bad movie. But it didn't happen in a movie. It happened to me. That was the shocking part. Me?! I mean, I'm no "pleaser." I'm not afraid of someone thinking I'm a difficult woman. My mantra is "Do no harm and take no shit." And yet, here I was, trembling in a "safe house," while telling my sister that a man had trapped me and assaulted me. It was all so dark.

Now we were both upset, our babies were screaming, and the trip was ruined. We talked about calling the police. The legality or illegality of it all was totally unclear to me. I knew he didn't rape me, but I also knew that I was terrified that he *would* rape me. What were the rules for the in-between? The Me Too vernacular was not yet in our airstream, so I didn't have the tools to do anything but, well, hide from this creep. All I wanted was to get home and get over it.

This was not the first time I had experienced sexual misconduct, but it was definitely the most traumatizing. When I was in college, one of the many jobs I had to survive in New York was as a hostess at a subterranean Upper West Side nightclub. I worked there for two weeks, with long shifts every night until three A.M., and when it was time to collect my money, the sleazy GM said if I wanted to get paid, I'd have to French kiss him first. Miserably, with my mouth closed tightly, I kissed him on the lips. Then I grabbed my money and ran. It was awful, and I never went back to work there again. It never occurred to me to tell anyone. The experience simply got filed away as "disgusting behavior women have to deal with—especially in the hospitality industry."

When Mario Batali was accused of being a sexual predator— which happened about a year after the LA hotel suite—the only thing that surprised me was that anyone was surprised. I'd spent countless nights on the third floor of the Spotted Pig, which will now go down in history as "the Rape Room." It's where I first met Heath Ledger (too sweet for this earth) and Gwyneth Paltrow (very cool), and where I made a lot of the cheffy connections I needed as a food writer at *New York* magazine. While I never witnessed any of the alleged abuse—such as Batali groping and kissing a woman who was passed-out drunk—everyone knew the third floor was a lawless den of drugs, sex, and sin. In my social circle, the knowledge that the Kings of the Kingdom behaved like scumbags was as well-known as their chargrilled burger with Roquefort. So you just kinda kept your antennae up. At least I did. See? I am not naive.

As Me Too gained even more momentum over the months, close friends urged me to "out" the powerful man, and consequent to the cultural shift, I felt slightly more equipped to think about it. One day, after dropping Hazel off at preschool, I called the only high-profile attorney I knew for advice. Let's call him Michael Wagner. Michael was a cute, single, big-time lawyer whom I met in the past via Tinder. His reputation as a killer in the courtroom preceded him, and his reputation as a good catch with great hair delighted him. Mike and I went out a couple times, but the only thing that blossomed was a nice, platonic friendship—and a direct line to a ferocious attorney who would always have my back.

As I waited for Mike to pick up the phone, I felt so anxious about putting the story into the universe in the context of litigation, even confidentially to a person whom I trusted, that I had to hang up on the second ring. I took a beat. I tried to locate the closest bathroom, worried I'd have to run there mid-call. I sat myself down on a stranger's front stoop and collected myself. Several deep breaths later, I felt centered enough to call Mike again.

Upon hearing the sound of my voice, he put his other appointments on hold, and graciously gave me his undivided attention. While circling the same block over and over by foot, I explained the story, from beginning to end. I was in such a zone that the world could have exploded in front of my face and I would not have noticed. And maybe it was about to.

We talked for an hour. The quiver in my voice never smoothed out. Straightaway, Mike confirmed that he thought I had a solid case, but it would have to go through California's legal system— because that's the state where the incident happened. The thought of litigation across the country, against a man with unlimited funds, especially as a single mom with no extra time or money, was insurmountably daunting. Mike was happy to help me look into it and find me counsel there, if I wanted him to. We ended the phone call with his assurance that he was there for me if I needed anything.

I gave it a few weeks—a lot of long walks, a lot of long phone calls with close friends. Every day now, famous and successful men were being alleged and convicted of sexual misconduct. This was the time to strike; my case would be buried under far more high-profile reports with names like Louis C.K., Matt Lauer, and James Franco. With so many bigger scandals than mine circling the headlines, maybe I could take down the powerful man without seeing any of it in the press.

So, why didn't I?

I'll be real with you. The overwhelming fear was about retaliation. One cannot begin to predict how powerful men with aggressive tendencies, who assault women, are going to behave. I had a daughter to think about and worried that poking the beast was, among other things, putting my family in danger.

And then there were the trappings of my brain. There was a small part of me that wondered—not if my memory was accurate, I knew exactly what had happened in that suite—but if I had overreacted to it. Couldn't one argue that he was just . . . hitting on me? Was that such a crime? He wanted me, and he assumed I wanted him too, even if I didn't realize it yet. Did I really need to set the world on fire for that? But here's the counterargument there: I've been hit on a lot in my life. Never before, however, had it entailed being held in a room against my will and humped, while I was trying to do my job, with my four-month-old baby down the road.

What contorted my brain even worse was this: I worried people would say that I asked for it. I hate that my mind went there. It's so cliché. But it's the truth. I was a lifelong flirt. "Kind of a whore," remember? In my twenties I was a wild-hearted party girl. The subtitle of my memoir, years later, was *My Messy Affairs In and Out of the Kitchen*. Emphasis on the words "messy" and "affairs." Now, I was a well-known love and sex writer whose day job entailed collecting stories about blow jobs and rim jobs. So, yeah, surely there was enough dirt on me to argue that I was a slut who sent mixed messages. At least that's what the shame-demons inside my head said.

The fighter in me, however, had a competing impulse. If nothing else, I had truth on my side. There were no cracks in my story. I could show the texts from him insisting we meet in the hotel suite.

There had to be security cameras around. If there weren't cameras inside the room, they were at least in the hallway where I ran out crying. And what about the valet guys? They saw me escape the hotel in a disoriented state of fear. But . . . who was going to risk their job for me? The key witness would probably be the publicist. She knew the whole story moments after it happened. A call log would prove we talked right away. Then again, I had no reason whatsoever to believe she would support me. It all felt so ill-fated.

Every single time I thought about litigation, I felt a heart attack, a panic attack, and a puke attack coming. My blood pressure, my stomach, my nervous system . . . everything broke down when I contemplated going public or taking any action. The decision tormented me. One half of me felt strongly entitled to keeping this thing private for the happiness and health of myself and my family, and the other half felt deeply responsible for other women's safety, and the greater good, and also, FUCK THAT GUY. All the voices in my head were battling it out day and night, and as I tried to raise my daughter alone, it was not where I wanted my very limited energy and resources to go.

In the end, the only thing I knew for sure was that Me Too-ing him felt like a dark and scary alley that I was desperate not to walk down. So I didn't. I stayed silent.

Once Me Too was everywhere, and the conversation was at least slightly destigmatized though no less disturbing, I contacted the powerful man's publicist to have lunch. I saw that she was in New York for a few weeks with another client. With some distance between the trauma and our chopped salads, I thought we could talk honestly about what had happened. I wasn't looking for an apology or any accountability or even some restitution, although I damn well deserved all of it. What I hoped for was a fully transparent conversation, with open minds and open hearts, between two adult women. Maybe, I thought, clearing the air in a positive way would help me move on, as I still had constant flashbacks to that afternoon.

The publicist chose a formal French restaurant in midtown New York, set in lush greenery and distressed brick, and as I turned the corner to walk inside, I had to consciously swallow my own vomit. Somehow I suppressed the throw-up enough times that it passed. Before I checked in with the hostess, I ducked into the bathroom to splash some cold water on my face and place a mint in my mouth, and as I dried my hands, they were shaking so bad under the automated machine that the hot air kept missing my fingers. So I wiped them on my skirt, which I'd made sure was ankle-length.

We hugged an awkward "Nice to finally meet you" hello. We sat across from each other cordially. I was visibly uneasy. She ordered the crudités.

Without waiting for the right moment, I asked: "Do you still rep him?"

"I do," she said confidently, quickly changing the subject.

She pulled out a shiny iPad to show me some images of new clients, and chipperly asked if my daughter liked Disney stars.

"Um, yeah, she does," I said, crestfallen, pretending I had something in my eye so that she couldn't see the runaway tear.

I did not touch my lunch. Nor did she introduce Hazel to any Disney stars.

Every few months since, I've googled the powerful man to see if anyone has come out with a sexual misconduct allegation against him, because if they did, I would be the first person to openly stand beside them. There is no way I'm the only person he's violated— though I imagine he has a very competent team managing such accusations, as it often goes. He's only gotten more moneyed and more successful over the years. I stopped interviewing famous people, for the most part. Maybe someday I'll say his name. Maybe it will always be too much. For now, the best I can do is tell this story and hope it makes someone, somewhere, feel a little less alone.

eighteen

Sam

A soft sun was beaming in through the windows of Vinegar Hill House, a *très* Brooklyn restaurant. I was sipping a Bloody Mary with extra olives at the bar. It was a pretty springtime morning, and my parents were babysitting Hazy so that I could go on a first date. When the café's front door squeaked open, I swiveled my head around to see who it was, and the sun was so blinding I had to squint to make sure the silhouette was the man I'd been waiting for.

He was indeed the man I'd been waiting for. And he was walking toward me.

"Hey!" I said, rising up from the barstool, not shaking his hand, which would have been the appropriate thing to do, but instinctively hugging him hello. "I'm Alyssa. Good to meet you."

"Sam," he said, hugging me back, not reluctantly, with a soft,

deep voice. He was both sexier and taller than I had imagined—
which in the world of online dating happens approximately never.

When Hazel was six months old, I joined Tinder, spontaneously
creating a profile that read *Single Mom in a very uncomplicated situation*. (In other words: no ex-husband or baby daddy drama.) The
first guy I met was obsessed with Jesus, the next with cunnilingus.
Neither impressed me much. But *Sam*. Even his name breathed ease.

He pulled up a barstool next to me like he was out of a Western and not a row house in Greenpoint, then politely nodded to
the bartender. "I'll have what she's having." He was wearing a vintage Johnny Cash T-shirt that I knew was all beat-up not because he
paid for the distressed look but because he'd probably had the thing
since high school and worn it ten thousand times before that day.
That was so much hotter to me than some Theory men's top, not
that this scrappy documentary filmmaker dude would know what
Theory was.

"Should we get some food, too?" he asked. *Passionate. Generous.
Hungry.* His pale blue eyes were strikingly kind and he smelled like
a bar of plain white soap and maybe half a cigarette. Normally, the
answer would be no. When you're a single working mother, you
must be a meticulous custodian of your own time, so I never agreed
to meet anyone for more than one drink, not even my best friends.
But bending the rules to get to know Sam seemed worth it. And
whatever, I wanted to stay for a while. He was calm and I was kooky
and the alchemy was there.

We ordered the lemon pancakes, the restaurant's famous fried
potatoes, and another round of Bloody Marys, with the works. He,
too, loved an olive.

Then came the requisite first date small talk, which was not tedious in this case but quite lovely. I learned that Sam took the bus to our date. *Gritty.* He went to a very good college that typically attracted ski bums and trust fund babies. *Interesting.* And his favorite food was a blueberry cake that his maternal grandmother, Minnie, always made for him on his birthday. *Sweet.* He learned that my parents, who now officially went by "Dodo" (my mother) and "Baba" (my father), lived on the same floor as me, in a building right down the block in DUMBO. We talked about our siblings, who were our best friends, and when he spoke of his family, I could tell he was a man who was not afraid of togetherness or closeness, and that compounded with the fact that he looked like a six-foot-tall and free-of-meth Jesse Pinkman seriously got me going.

Of course, I couldn't go too long without making things awkward.

The first terrible thing I said was that, per Facebook, we had one mutual friend in common. It was a guy who I grew up with in Longmeadow and who I once "blew in the Unitarian church parking lot." To that little nugget, Sam nodded politely, informing me that this person was not just a random acquaintance but a close friend. "Well, don't feel weird about it or anything. It was a pretty sloppy hookup," I elaborated, as if Sam wanted to keep this particular thread going for one second longer.

Believe it or not, the next thing I said was arguably worse.

"So, you got a thing for single moms, huh?"

I mean, what is wrong with me?! I thought: *How about next I tell him that Nordstrom Rack officially broke up with me because I returned over 90 percent of my purchases last year?* No, seriously. I got a letter from

Nordstrom's corporate office saying they were "ending our relationship." And I'd actually been really sad about it lately. Oh. I know.

Maybe I should tell Sam that I always know I'm getting a cold when there's a canker sore on my tongue.

Or that I'm a 24-7 bathrobe person.

That I used to have great legs but I have no idea what happened to them?

Wait, is he interested in functional constipation?

What about my teenage trip to Auschwitz?

Sam—as refined as a crescent moon—teetered between charmed and stunned by the single mom question. Charmed and Stunned being his new baseline for all things with me, moving forward. We had already messaged each other a little bit online, so he knew I had a baby, and he knew I'd used an anonymous sperm donor to make her, but he didn't know any other details. And it was in his wonderful response that I knew, conclusively, I not only wanted him but I liked him:

"I think you're the first one. But yeah, I'm down. I'm totally down."

Suddenly our barstools were positioned closer beside each other. We kept chatting. Sam was not a guy who liked to talk about himself very much, but luckily I was skilled at asking personal questions. Mostly, I was intrigued by his family. They were all Mainers. Coastal Maine. Rural Maine. Simple Maine. Farming Maine. Fancy Maine. He said his dad bought a dilapidated shack, in a town called Verona Island, back in the early eighties, and as he painstakingly built the family something more sustainable, they all slept on mattresses in the hallways and everyone used an outhouse. Before I could fish around for any more details, Sam led the conversation in a different direction.

Without saying it in so many words, Sam wanted to let me know that nothing about my motherhood felt fraught to him. He told me that within his closest family and friends, they'd experienced one pregnancy through surrogacy, another through egg donation, and there was an adoption in the works. Because he had sisters and sisters-in-law and lots of aunts of all ages, he was open and enlightened when it came to fertility, and that was really refreshing.

"Thanks so much for telling me all that," I said, a smile spreading across my face like butterfly wings. It wasn't like I needed a guy to tell me he was okay with my choices, but I also didn't realize how comforting it would feel to hear it.

There was one more thing.

This was something Sam had never told anybody before, and certainly never imagined being published in a book someday, but here goes: Sam donated sperm in college. Mostly because it seemed like a quick and easy way to help families in need. He was, after all, doing *the thing,* all the time, anyway. But it wasn't a pure act of kindness, either. I mean, some ski bums need beer money.

Sam seemed relieved to confess this out loud, for the first time, to a real person, who happened to be the very right person to receive it. I loved this new detail about him. I loved that he trusted me with it. I loved that he owned it. I loved thinking that because of him, a family was now complete, and that he, too, would have to live with some question marks around our biological ties.

The craziest part, though, was that Sam had worked with California Cryobank, the same sperm bank I used for Hazel. That kind of blew my mind, and I'll tell you why. When CBS was developing that half-hour comedy about my journey into motherhood via an anonymous sperm donor, an executive there kept suggesting that the Alyssa character serendipitously meet and fall in love with her anonymous sperm donor. I always fought back on that note, insisting that would *never* happen in real life. Furthermore, why propagate the notion that anyone who uses a sperm donor secretly dreams of finding him and being with him because they really *can't* do this alone and secretly just want to be *saved* by a man. I always found that "take" to be tone-deaf. It insulted me. And yet. Well, shit. Had I gone the "blond hair, blue eyes, boyish soccer player" route—which I had not—this guy actually could have been my daughter's biological father.

We were now shoulder to shoulder at the bar, and our knees gently touched under the table.

We sipped our Bloody Marys and continued to peel back our layers. Despite the fact that he was an all-American boy who'd grown up on a farm, and I was an oversharing yenta who'd grown up at T. J. Maxx, we had a lot in common. He was scraping by as a cinematographer but had bigger dreams as a film director. I yammered on about the evildoers in Hollywood kicking me in the stomach— while pregnant, no less—because the only thing I like holding more than a Bloody Mary is a grudge. We were both rebels who knew our limits, drifters who could never stray too far from our families. We were deep, but not damaged. Sensitive, but not sad. He supported Bernie Sanders—and I supported Andy Cohen. He had made a film about Native Americans who were stripped of their citizenship— and I wrote a book about being engaged to a Top Chef who was famous for his fedoras. His dream was to build an icehouse for ice-fishing in the winter; my dream was to take four bubble baths a day like Tom Ford. He was deeply aware of the suffering of the world; I was deeply aware of his very fine lips.

After three hours at the restaurant, I needed to get back to my daughter. Sam asked if he could walk me home. I registered his request, and then pleasantly nodded. Though a piece of my heart knew I was already there.

nineteen

Verona Island

Are you *sure* they realize you're bringing home a Jewish girl, with a baby, who you only met four weeks ago?" I asked Sam while he carried a sleeping Hazel and my suitcase at Bangor Airport.

"Yeah. Why? They can't wait to meet you guys," he said, like nothing, no biggie, NBD, as we walked out to his sage-green Volkswagen station wagon parked outside the baggage claim. A car in which Hazel had already, more than once, projectile vomited—which, in my opinion, was a little too soon.

I was on edge. I hadn't had much positive interaction with my boyfriends' parents in the past. One ex's mother once asked me to reimburse her for a throwaway razor I used in their shower to shave my armpits; another boyfriend's father got arrested, and then asked me to falsely testify that the cops had called me a kike. And don't forget the family that pretended I was dead for three years.

Sam had arrived at his parents' place in Maine a few days earlier. It was June, the weekend of his thirty-fifth birthday, and in conjunction with that, everyone was coming to town for an outdoor Dolly Parton concert. Two of Sam's siblings would be there, along with their spouses and children. They all had tickets to the show. These were big Dolly Parton people, and I had no idea what to make of that. All I really knew about Dolly Parton was that she had those famous bazoombas.

Inside Sam's car, country music played on the radio. The old twangy stuff. Further evidence that the Russells were going to be a bunch of bighearted hillbillies who lived in the backwoods, and I was totally there for it. This could be my Moira Rose from *Schitt's Creek* moment—she was my exemplary role model after all.

All I really knew was that after a few hours at home with his family—presumably after telling them that he had "met someone"— Sam phoned me and suggested that Hazel and I join everyone on Verona Island, which was on Maine's MidCoast, at the head of Penobscot Bay, about forty minutes from Bangor Airport. He had tickets on hold for us (for the plane and the Dolly concert) and really wanted to buy them. When he told me this, I was folding laundry on my floor and my mother was feeding Hazel a huge smushed-up matzo ball in her high chair. His proposition felt a little *extra*. I mean, if nothing else, who would want some random baby at their house?

"*Go!*" my mother pushed when I put the phone down to confer with her. She flapped her hand in the air as if to shoo us away with her blessing. "Get out of here, go have fun!"

She hadn't met Sam yet—we'd only been on a few dates, I might reiterate—but she had a good feeling about him. These last few weeks had been exciting for me, and she saw the spring in my step. Either that, or she assumed he came from old money. My mother was convinced that she clicked best with Old Money, often espousing the quote, "Old money's the same as no money." And if that wasn't the thought process, I bet she thought: *We'll at least get a decent country house out of it.* Finally, some real estate from one of these schmucks.

Fast-forward a day and Sam was picking us up from Bangor Airport.

"All right, all right." I'd shrugged with amusement to his nonchalance about introducing us to his world so fast as he fastened Hazel into a car seat. "Just sayin' . . . it seems like *a lot*. But you know them better than me!"

Far be it from me to call any situation crazy. It's not like I was some provincial thinker when it came to dating; I mean, I brought my seven-month-old daughter on all our dates after the first one. Before I knew the details of Sam's last relationship, he knew the details of my breastfeeding stretch marks. Before we talked dirty, we talked dirty diapers. Obviously, I liked relationships that were inside out and upside down, that moved at their own speed with their own rules of emotional acceleration, and that's definitely the way Sam and I were operating. So I tried to stay calm and present, open to wherever the wind would blow us.

Never, however, did I imagine that the wind would blow us to the place that came next.

On the drive from the airport to his parents' house, I tried to assess the area. I had never really been to the state before, but I was a third-generation New Englander by blood. I understood things like little post offices, town greens, church suppers, Trump/Pence signs abutting Oprah Winfrey/Michelle Obama signs, Natty Light, stores that sold "wedding gowns *and* guns." From preppies to townies, nothing was so out of the ordinary to me—it was just a little more rural there, a bit grainier. "You call 'em grinders in these parts?" I asked, trying to sound all street with my sandwich colloquialisms.

"Nope. We say I-talians."

"Cool," I said. *Cool.*

Sam drove quietly and contently with the radio on, turning the dial from Willie Nelson to NPR and back. "I'm really happy you girls are here," he said, turning his head toward me, smiling. *He is so hot and cool and low-key* played on loop in my brain as we drove. I asked if his grandmother Minnie had baked him his favorite blueberry cake for his birthday, a detail he had forgotten he'd told me on our first date. He now seemed embarrassed for giving a shout-out to his grandma as part of his game. "Rumor has it, she did indeed make me the cake." He grinned shyly.

I asked what else we were going to do for the three days we were meant to stay there—my way of digging for more details on the fam. He suggested a little hiking, some beaching, a visit to his aunt Kelly's waterfront café in Castine, an overnight at the family's little cabin on Lake Alamoosook, maybe a bit of canoeing. It was all so quaint-sounding. *This might be too much,* I thought, looking back at Hazel, who hadn't been changed since the airport in New York and whose onesie, no doubt, was oozing with saffron-yellow poop. And worse, me! I checked myself out in the punishing front seat mirror, which no one with any self-respect should ever do, and I saw a human Hebrew school. On her period. As well as two wiry and unleashed chin hairs. I needed an electrolysis—not a canoe. My skin had sunspots and problem areas everywhere and it all made me feel like a cold plate of leftover couscous, not some luscious hot-shit writer. What I'm trying to say is this: I have never looked so *unWASPy*.

As Sam made a left turn onto a long, gravel road called Russell Lane, I looked at him with horror.

"Wait. Hold on. You guys have your own fucking street?" I yelped.

"Nah, it's not like that. Everyone in Maine has their own fucking street." But, reader, he did not say "fucking." Because he's classier than me. See? That's precisely the point. Sam had not prepared me for this.

Also. I lied. There were three chin hairs.

Russell Lane was pure paradise. The first vignette my eyes took in was a shimmery little pond with lily pads and a small vintage rowboat tied to an old relaxed dock. Past the pond was a handsome red barn that housed classic tractors on one side and a pretty green-house on the other. With mounting awe, I took in the acres and acres of meadows and gardens that came next. They were the most glori-ous gardens I had ever seen in my life: peonies, irises, poppies, lilacs, to name a few (and let's be real: to name the only flowers I know the names of). These were epic gardens that would make Mary Ol-iver quiver and Martha Stewart cry, and I suspected Sam's mother designed, cultivated, and took care of all of them. Sam put the VW into fourth, and drove ahead slowly. I didn't know if I should laugh or cry. We weren't even at the main house yet.

That's when I noticed the silky blue sky. *Universe, are you kid-ding me with this sky?* It was glittering with bluebirds, swallows, goldfinches, doves, and sparrows (again, the only birds I know the names of). Sam added, in his hot, cool, and low-key way—which was starting to make me want to strangle him—to look out for the occasional eagle, too.

To the right were blueberry fields and a swimming pool, and in the far distance, I could see a rolling river set against looming purple mountains. Down by the river, I spotted a post-and-beam guest cabin tucked into the woods like a heavy nap in a Pendleton quilt, and I thought, *There ya go, Ma*.

The main house itself was lovely and modest. A happy home. A home of chicken potpie and Terry Gross and eucalyptus Epsom salts and the morning paper and just enough love and history to keep things interesting. It was not some huge, fancy farmhouse, thank God. I mean, thank *no one*. Sam said they were all pretty much agnostics.

Before I knew it, two adorable dogs, Rufus and Gracie, and an older couple who looked like Meg Ryan and Harrison Ford were sailing out the front door. "Jeje and Pops," Sam's parents, were greeting us with open arms and the warmest smiles, eager to welcome my daughter and me into their lives.

And for the first time ever, I was truly speechless.

twenty

Dolly and Doug

The Russells were as kind as they were attractive and it was going to be very hard to hate them.

Everyone was around that weekend, coming and going at "the Farm," as the family called it. Maine had warmed itself up and its good people were rising from hibernation. As such, I imagined that for decades now the Russells' inner circle knew that Jeje's gardens promised to awaken the soul like no other, that her flowers could kiss you the way you needed to be kissed, even if you didn't know it. Springtime was definitely the time to swing on by.

Jeje was a Virgo like my mom, which gave me a head start in understanding her. Although, their Virgoisms manifested in very different ways. For example, for my entire adult life, my mother had compulsively called or texted me at 5:49 A.M. to let me know that she did not die in her sleep. (She is, and always has been, in perfect health.) Jeje, on the other hand, had labeled glass jars of oats, almond flour, candied pecans, and dried apricots, and was so organized that there was nothing—no mosquito bite, no surprise party, no lemonade stand—that she did not have a "department" for. Non-Virgo-related, Jeje was also a lot like Sam, or should I say, Sam was a lot like her: steady, gentle, and good. I found her to be very special. She also had impeccable timing for delivering the line, "Who's ready for a drink?"

Sam's dad, Pops, was warmhearted, intelligent, and unbelievably generous. He'd give you the skin off his back, and then write *you* a check for taking it. He was a lover and a doer, and at seventy years old had constant projects going on at the Farm and his other properties in town. Pops made most of the dads I knew look like complete couch potatoes, dullards, or nincompoops. And while he was nothing like my own father, whose primary "project" in life was doing exactly as my mother, my sister, and I instructed (and thus could do no wrong as far as we were concerned), they were both world-class dads. And though it was far too early to apply this information to our situation, it did not go unnoticed that Sam had a stellar role model when it came to fatherhood.

Jeje and Pops had built this haven together from scratch. What looked to me like a sprawling estate straight out of *Town & Country* was forty years of saving, sacrificing, digging, excavating, building, learning, growing, and grit. The land was two hundred acres of pleasure born from struggle and as a result of that, it had a spirituality that money can't buy.

The days at the Farm were swirled with flurries of kids, dogs, neighbors, friends, bleeding-heart liberals, recovering Republicans, beekeepers, pie bakers, pot cookie ladies, local politicians, Reiki healers, and a ridiculous amount of aunts, uncles, cousins, and grand-parents, I nearly lost my mind trying to keep track of all of them.

Minnie was married to Ralph, Sam's grandpa, who called Hazel "lil bugga" and was everyone's favorite man. (I fell hard for him my-self, even though, by then, he was well into his battle with dementia.) I met a worldly Uncle Joe whom some called Jon, a cousin Louie whom Jon called Stanley, a middle-schooler named Emerson who was a ski (or was it sailing?) champion, and a brother-in-law, Adam, whom Ralph called Cream Puff. Cream Puff was a super-successful, Scarsdale-raised, type A Jew who had broken them all in nicely for me. He was married to Sam's sister, Carrie Russell, who was even prettier than the *Felicity* actress Keri Russell—whom I see all the time in Brooklyn and is drop-dead gorgeous. No one should ever be pret-tier than her. Sam's brother, Todd, was hip and unexpectedly fringe, and Todd's wife, Jessica—who was injured in a car accident when she was eighteen, and left with paralysis from the chest down—was the funniest woman I'd ever met, and this is coming from someone who has interviewed Maya Rudolph *and* Molly Shannon. Jessica was also one of Sam's besties, so I really wanted her approval specifically.

What did all these generations and iterations of people wearing L.L.Bean (and sometimes Vince.) have in common? They were all wonderful. Like, *wonderful*. It was surreal. I felt like I was on Ecstasy. Everyone treated Hazel and me like long-lost relatives. I mean, every single person was warm and engaging to the point where I needed to hide in the bathroom and call my most catty and bitchy friends in New York just to hear that someone—anyone—had fallen apart.

Plus, there was Sam. I quickly realized why he had brought us to the Farm so soon, although I think it was subconscious on his part.

It wasn't to show off. Mainers don't show off. It wasn't to flaunt his family's spectacular oasis. No, Sam needed us to see the Farm so that we could see *him*. And it worked. I saw that he was a product of pure poetry, that his religion was clean, crisp air and a mountainous view, that he was well equipped to handle life's inevitable complexities but he himself was happiest with the simple things. The Farm made me like, and desire, Sam even more (and I already liked and desired him quite a bit). But what would happen when Sam saw me, all flesh and bones, too? My natural habitat was not always pretty, and the poetry was sometimes impure. *Is that going to be okay?* I started to wonder.

On our second afternoon there, while Hazel was happy as a clam playing with Sam's nieces and nephews, a family friend asked if I wanted to pick some herbs with her in the vegetable garden. The sentence was so wholesome that it was almost exotic. I mean, I've gone with friends to AA meetings, breast-augmentation consults, speed-dating sushi, and holy shrines where Hasids and tourists collectively pray for miracles—but never to pick herbs in a vegetable garden together.

Over some cilantro—or maybe it was mint?—the family friend held both of my hands, looked me in the eye, and told me that the Russells were "the best people in the world."

Her intentions were innocent; I think she wanted to sell them to me because she had heard that Sam liked us so much. But because I am human and was a single mom with a baby, and I'd experienced more romantic heartbreak and disappointment than anyone should in one lifetime, what I heard was this: *These are the best people in the world and you are not good enough for them.*

That is absolutely not what she said, and it's not what she meant, but the voices in our head are unreliable narrators. I tried to swat away any uprising of an inferiority complex, because once you go there, it's tough to come back. Plus, my insecurity just wasn't grounded in reality. No one at the Farm treated us like *less than*. If anything, we were treated like *more than*. They all had so much admiration for my life as a writer and an author. All the women wiped away happy, emotional tears when I told them the story of me and Hazy. One aunt, Jeannie, gave Hazel the necklace she was wearing right off her neck; another aunt, Lisa, gave me a hello hug that made my heart want to burst. We were nothing but wanted and respected there—why was that so hard for me to accept?

Sam's paternal grandmother, Gran, a ninety-something matriarch of all matriarchs, was the one I was most nervous about impressing. Her late husband was an esteemed town doctor in Castine, and she herself was a woman of status, though deeply humble and anti-snob. She looked like Kennebunkport but preferred the Salvation Army. She was a relentless social activist with connections to former presidents, senators, and all sorts of big Maine names. But it didn't matter who you were, and it was probably better if you were a nobody, because Gran was good to everybody. She was kind, playful, and compassionate. There is so much more I could say about Gran, but even this paragraph would overwhelm her, because it's starting to sound like bragging.

Gran had so many grandchildren and great-grandchildren that, traditionally, her weekend visits were more like "drive-bys" if she wanted to fit everyone in. And she was very fair like that. When Hazel and I first met her, we were transfixed. Neither of us would leave her side; we were like hungry little Ashkenazi puppies. After about twenty minutes getting to know each other a little bit, Gran had to take off. She had a tag sale to get to. But before she drove away—famous for her Irish exits, even though she was Scottish ancestrally—Gran asked if Hazel and I wanted to take a quick picture together, whipping out an old camera. "Of course!" I beamed, honored by the request. So we gave Sam the camera and Gran, Hazel, and I all put our arms around each other. "Everyone say 'Hazel'!" sang Gran.

"But what if you never see us again?" I asked, holding Hazel, after posing for the picture. "What will you do with the photo? I mean, Sam and I *just* started dating. I wouldn't put this in a polished silver frame just yet . . . maybe like, on the side of the fridge . . . tacked under a Hannaford magnet . . . that way we're more disposable. Ya know?"

Why on earth I chose Sam's distinguished grandmother to express my budding angst about my new relationship is beyond me. But it would take a lot more than a little love-life strife to rattle Gran.

"Aw, well, in that case I'll be even happier that we took a picture together so I can remember you two."

Mainers are so sensible.

Gran actually reminded me of my mother's mother, Dorothy Temkin Pava, the matriarch of all matriarchs in *my* family. She had recently died in her nineties, quietly and peacefully in her own bed, after having a massive stroke. When she was alive, she was *also* strong, elegant, honest, and wise. She, too, loved a tag sale. After my parents moved to New York in 1998, my mother would drive back to Massachusetts monthly to meet up with my auntie Ellie and my grandma, to go "tagging," then they'd meet up with my other aunts, Susan and Barbara, for a quick coffee or tuna melt at a diner. Like Gran, my grandmother had a gaggle of grandkids and never missed a beat with any of us. She kept up with all our simchas and shenanigans. Although, she did die thinking I was highly likely a lesbian, thanks to the sperm donor thing. We could never convince her otherwise, but that's okay.

It did make me kinda sad, though, comparing the two. My grandmother had an extremely hard life. Her husband, my mother's father, Lazar Temkin, committed suicide, and left her with six young kids. They were dirt-poor. She did not know how to drive a car or write a check, and oftentimes she'd have to cook for the six kids with whatever scraps of food she could find. My grandmother was a warrior, though, and they made do, and her kids had joyful lives . . . and then her youngest son, the beloved baby of the family, my uncle Mikey, committed suicide too.

My mother did not, and still does not, like to talk about the suicides. She used to say it was because they had to lie about the cause of death to the funeral homes so that her father and brother could be buried in Jewish cemeteries. She said that's why no one ever talked about it, to not get found out. But I think it's much more connected to shame.

Anyway, I'm not saying Gran did not have her share of grief or hardships—and much like my grandmother, if she did, she wasn't going to dwell on it. I'm just saying that, in juxtaposing these two marvelous women, Gran's life as a whole seemed so much more enchanted. And so much less painful.

The night before the Dolly Parton concert, Todd and Jessica suggested we go out for some drinks. Everyone grew up in the area and knew which bars to go to if we wanted to dance, play pool, eat wings, or get into a bar fight with a woman named Mo or man named Shirley.

Carrie and her husband, Adam, aka Cream Puff, were staying home with their (also wonderful!) kids, and offered to babysit Hazel at the Farm so that Sam and I could have a night off. I felt funny telling them that this would be the first time that I'd left my daughter with anyone but my parents. They probably had a roster of reliable babysitters, like most normal families, back in their Boston suburb. Carrie insisted, though, and I was very grateful. Sam and I had never been out at night without a sleeping baby in a stroller.

We chose a roadside bar that had a mix of Ping-Pong and ex-prisoners, and it was actually very romantic there. It was a fun night out, but I was a little watered down, for me at least. It was impossible to keep up with Jessica's genius wit and overall magnetism, and I think I was still in shock over the utopia of the Farm. One part of me kept thinking, *What the hell do you think you're doing there?* And the other part of me was like, *This is exactly the lifestyle you deserve.*

After some very heavy four-dollar-wine pours, we all went outside for a smoke. The only problem was, I never smoked. And the reason I never smoked was because of a very serious condition: Cigarettes give me pimples. It happens every single time. And these pimples are psychopathic monsters. They're the kind you can see from the corner of your eye, the kind that pulsate and throb, the kind that last a few weeks and then leave a lifetime pockmark. Whenever my sister or I have a pimple of this caliber, my dad calls it "Doug." I didn't want a Doug for the Dolly Parton concert tomorrow, but I didn't want to seem like a drag, either. Normally, I would have worked through the pimple dilemma out loud, but I was also afraid of appearing too vain to Sam's crew.

Mainers are not vain.

All they needed to know was that Sam was dating a really cool chick. I needed to present as a really cool chick. That was the bottom line. So I made the emergency calculation that I'd rather have acne than be an asshole.

The next day I woke up with Sam, Hazel, and Doug. The pimple, in the middle of my left cheek—bull's-eye, baby—was a whopper and it killed. A blanket of crackly taupe makeup would only make it look worse, so I didn't even bother. My only option was to own it.

Try owning a glistening purple pimple while making breakfast next to Carrie Russell who is prettier than Keri Russell, and who makes the fluffiest and creamiest of scrambled eggs. To show that I was a team player, I offered to prepare some oatmeal. But I didn't know where any of the right pots, pans, or utensils were, and I was overly worried about messing up a Virgo's kitchen flow, and suddenly I couldn't even remember how to make oatmeal anyway. So I made nothing, and no one noticed. I tried to brew another pot of coffee for everyone, at least, but I also couldn't figure out how their espresso percolator thing worked. At every turn, I felt like a klutz and a moron. The room smelled like bacon and I wanted to remind Hazel that bacon was not kosher and we very much were. Then Jeje quietly mentioned that it was turkey bacon, because she knew we didn't eat pork. *OMG, she was so thoughtful.* There were crossword puzzles and fresh berries in bowls, and no one was gossiping, fighting, or complaining, and I couldn't think of anything else to say, other than, "I am so ugly compared to you all." Though I kept that inside. And kind of just faded from the meal. Also, I was very hungover.

A few hours later, Sam found Hazel and me reading a Mo Willems book out in the back cabin. And by reading a Mo Willems book, I mean taking deep breaths and wondering if we should go home.

"What are you girls doing down here?" he asked tenderly.

"Just taking a little break, I guess," I replied, giving him a weary look that implied I was not necessarily okay.

"Sam?" I said. "This is a lot. You guys are perfect. And you might have figured out by now that I am borderline perfect-intolerant. I just . . . I don't . . . I'm not sure I fit in here."

Sam listened. But he wasn't going to let me rewrite the truth. "Everyone loves you, Lys. They already love you more than they love me. And trust me, we're *not* perfect. . . . No family is perfect."

"What did you like about me when we first met? On our Bloody Mary date. What did you see in me?" I don't know why, but I needed some reassurance.

He didn't have to think about it too long.

"I walked in and you were glowing. And because of your glow, everything around you was radiating. And I thought if I had the chance to be with someone who made life so luminous, I would be a lucky man."

It felt like the nicest thing anyone had ever said to me.

Sam asked if I wanted him to take Hazel outside for a little bit so I could have some time to myself. I nodded. He swooped her up and we all hugged tight, the three of us. Then I watched as he took her over to his favorite spot by the river, to sit on a big old swing that Ralph had built by hand when Sam was a young boy, a swing that looked out at the big rocks and rolling waves. Maybe they'd see an eagle.

In the cabin, I thought very hard about what I was feeling, and what was beneath those feelings. I knew I was different from the Russells, and I don't care how evolved or self-possessed you are, it's not easy being different. I'd felt different from most "normal people" my entire life, and sometimes that made me feel like a rock star, and sometimes it made me feel like a freak. There will always be something in my molecules telling me that no one will ever understand me, and that I am better off alone. But that framework is probably why I have access to so many emotions, and it's undoubtedly the reason I'm a good writer, friend, sister, and mother. Not all of us can live so comfortably in the bosom of pathos but I can.

As for my family's beautiful and fragmented past, our scars and secrets truly cannot compete with the love and light that defined my childhood. And in the spirit of accurate reporting, just like I already envied the Russells, friends had always envied us. In high school, kids would line up at the front door of my house to eat my mother's homemade apple pie and talk and laugh about everything under the sun with her and me. My childhood friends treasured my mom's outspoken opinions and delighted in the eye rolls of my dad, who—when he was allowed to speak—was actually extremely funny. Like Carrie, my sister was also strikingly pretty and down-to-earth and multidimensional. And all my aunts, uncles, and cousins were Russell-level kind and generous too. My pity party had no merit. The material was thin. The Russells might be the best people in the world, but so were we.

Still, there was a bigger lesson to be learned.

I was a mother now. And I only had one chance of being a mom who believed in herself. In some ways, the Farm was the moment I had been training for my entire life. To be a self-actualized adult woman. To find nobility in my choices. To find humility in my flaws. To find spirituality in my big, fat pimp—No . . . Doug sucked. The point is, motherhood demanded a new kind of grace. *Motherhood demanded a new kind of grace.*

How would all this translate to my future with Sam? That was still unclear. It was still so early in our love story. I wasn't sure if we were soul mates; I wasn't even sure if we were falling in love. Honestly, I didn't even know if I believed in soul mates or falling in love anymore. There was no way I'd ever get engaged again. Marriage was off the table. And nice, stable monogamous couplehood just seemed so unmodern and un-me.

But as I walked toward him and Hazel, quietly feeding their souls while gazing out into the world, I knew that he and I could—and should—band together to survive it.

twenty-one

Stop Draggin' My Heart Around

S am was onstage with a random woman, badly singing the words "Baby, you'll come knocking on my front door . . ."

It was early fall and we were back in Maine for Sam's sister Abby's wedding at the Farm. He and I had been dating about seven months, and Hazel had just turned one. The three of us were inseparable, and she was the center of both of our universes.

Abby and her fiancé, Brian, were surfer-entrepreneurial types who lived in Santa Barbara and—though I didn't think it was possible—added a new layer of pure Russell magic to the mix. They were young and fun, and just boho-chic enough to be sexy and vulnerable and interesting. When Abby told me she had sleep issues that sometimes made her "a little cray," I almost kissed her on the lips for having at least one relatable imperfection.

After their rehearsal dinner, there was a talent show at the town hall in Castine, with Abby and Brian's friends and family performing goofy and sentimental acts in front of all the weekend wedding guests, an audience of two hundred or so. Fortunately, I was still "new" enough to the group that no one expected me to get onstage— totally not my kind of thing. I'd sooner die than do a corny singalong or participate in something like a flash mob dance. I seriously can't even be friends with someone whose best night ever includes karaoke.

A few acts in, a group of Sam and Abby's friends did a spoof of a "modern dance" performance, all *dramatique* and over-the-top. Everyone wore nude unitards, which were hilarious even without the ridiculous leaps and twirls. However, one of their best friends, Ryan, did not exactly fit into his. Unbeknownst to Ryan, his nude unitard clung to what must have been a ten-inch shlong. You couldn't look away. So let me set the table for you here: imagine a bunch of wholesome, mostly older, Good Samaritan Mainers pretending to be oohing and ahhing for the pirouettes and arabesques when really, no one could take their eyes off Ryan's bulging D. I couldn't help but think of all the kitschy shops in the area: Mainely Pottery. Mainely Antiques. Mainely Crystals. *Mainely Cock.*

Sam's duet came after the experimental dance ensemble. At the last minute, he told one of Abby's friends that he'd accompany her to "Stop Draggin' My Heart Around," but he hadn't had time to prac- tice and was not, despite his indie musician vibe, much of a natural- born singer. The performance was adorable, though technically . . . he was awful. Turns out my boyfriend who would never be tone- deaf when it came to the state of the world was a little bit tone-deaf when it came to Stevie Nicks and Tom Petty.

Everyone quickly forgot about the botched song, but Sam was embarrassed. It's pretty much his greatest fear to be any sort of spectacle, so he was regretful of the whole thing. He stayed close to me all night as I tried to distract him from himself by dazzling all his friends (especially Mr. "Stop Draggin' That Dick Around" Ryan) and getting us tipsy. Despite my attempts to turn the night around, we took off at a reasonable time, agreeing to rest up for the wedding tomorrow. While recapping the evening in bed, Sam took my face in his hands and told me he loved me.

I am almost positive he said "I love you," so that I wouldn't dump him after hearing him sing. But regardless, he said it. And I said it right back. I loved the man! He was everything I ever wanted in a partner. We supported each other. We desired each other. We trusted each other. Officially "in love," we both gazed at Hazel, who was sound asleep in a crib right next to our bed, and didn't try to hide our flowing tears of gratitude.

But Abby's wedding the next day marked an even bigger milestone for our relationship.

Under the warm, late-afternoon autumn sky, which would give way to a beautiful harvest moon (obviously!), Hazy and I took our seats in the crowd. The entire Farm had been transformed into a magnificently flowered fête, and Jeje had set up an ethereal pergola on a small hill by the cabin, all ferns and dahlias and fairy dust. Sam was in the processional and tucked away somewhere with the wedding party, so Hazel and I were on our own. We found a nice spot next to one of my favorite aunts of his—although they were all my favorite aunts of his—and Hazel sat on my lap like a buttercream cupcake with a unibrow.

When Lord Huron's "Fool for Love" started, everyone twisted around to watch the wedding commence. A few moments later,

Sam and his brother, Todd, walked down the aisle. They both looked devastatingly handsome . . . when suddenly my romantic haze was interrupted by my other Haze. She was yelling—literally, screaming—something at the top of her little lungs.

"Dada!" she yelped. "Dada!!!!"

What? Hazel! Dada?? No, Hazel, no! It's Sammy! It's just Sammy.

"Dada!" she hollered again, right at Sam, desperately needing him to look our way and make eye contact with her. She might as well have yelled, "Yo, Pops, we're over here!"

Finally he heard her. (I mean, everyone heard her. Gran, who won't even splurge on a high-end hearing aid, heard her.) He looked over to us, and smiled from ear to ear. He waved at Hazy and blew her a kiss, and kept walking down the aisle per his groomsman role.

"Dadaaah," she sighed, relieved. "Dadaaah."

The guests were all very charmed by my daughter's outburst. Minnie was giggling. All the aunts cooed. Now it was my turn to be embarrassed.

The truth was, it wasn't the first time Hazel had said the word "Dada." Sam and I kept pretending she was talking about "doggies" back in Brooklyn, who, in fairness, she sort of called "dadas" too. But we both knew what she meant when she looked at Sam, who was not a puppy, and said the word. We just weren't sure if it was okay to talk about it yet. Sure, we were in a very serious relationship and about to move in together, a precious little trio with a rhythm and a beat. But Sam becoming Hazel's dad was an epic thing, right? Didn't it require, oh, I don't know, mediation or meditation or couples counseling or a priest or Esther Perel?

I had no one to ask about this stuff. My single mom friends

were not interested in my fairy-tale romance and who could blame them? It was obnoxious. I belonged to one Single Mom by Choice Facebook group, a group that typically had hundreds of comments on everything from small-footprint Crock-Pots to organic eczema cures. But when I posted, "Anyone out there navigating a new boyfriend with a baby?" I got crickets. It was the only post in the history of a Facebook mom group that yielded zero opinions. Instant Pots were one thing, but Instant Dads? No one had a clue.

The truth is, I didn't need any advice. I knew what to do. Since having a baby, something had shifted inside. Life was less binary, and my emotions had softer edges. Could I be independent and free, while also finding immense joy in sharing a life with someone? Yup. All those feelings could exist at once. Could I stand by my conviction that Hazel and I did not need a man to thrive and survive in the world together—and yet, also thank God, with all my heart, for sending us Sam? Yes. So ultimately, what could have been the hardest, most complicated, most strife-ridden decision of my life— allowing a new man to become my daughter's father—was the most natural decision I ever made. With Sam, things always felt right. The three of us folded together like a beautiful braid, and I knew we were meant to be . . . *just be* . . . together.

As we packed up for Brooklyn and Hazel started Dada-ing again, I had to say something.

"Enough already! What do we do about this?" I said to Sam as straightforward as possible while he folded up his suit from the night before into his duffle (lest I fall in love with a man who owns a TUMI garment bag). "Hazel calling you . . . *you know* . . . Are you, like, cool with it?" As I awaited his response, it was a little hard for me to breathe.

He looked at her, and then he looked at me.

"Yes! Yes, I'm cool with it! Of course I'm cool with it!" His eyes were watery, his cheeks flushed. "It would be my greatest honor."

Sam and I both left that weekend in love, and fully surrendering to our happiness, not trapped by the confines of partnership and parenthood but, somehow, freed by it.

And just like that, my fatherless daughter had a dada.

twenty-two

Both Sides of a Breakup

My next-door neighbor Audra needed me to check on her husband, Harris, to make sure he had not killed himself.

Earlier that evening, Harris had confessed to Audra that he'd been entangled in a two-year-long sexual affair. His mistress was pregnant, and she was probably keeping the baby. Harris was a doctor, and she was originally his patient, and he was likely going to get fired from his practice because his partner had caught them sixty-nine-ing in an exam room. As if the story couldn't get any more scandalous, Harris was also likely going to lose his medical license because the partner was pissed. And no, Harris is not Hugh Grant in *The Undoing*. This story came first.

Upon being punched in the gut with this shocking and horrifying news, Audra packed up their teenage daughter, checked into a hotel, and told Harris to jump off a cliff and die. Then, a few hours later, as I boiled Sam and me some fettucine and stuck a tray of dinosaur chicken nuggets in the oven for Hazel, Audra was calling me worried that Harris would actually do the thing she commanded, and jump off a cliff (or more likely the Brooklyn Bridge) and die.

She was too angry to check on him herself, and it wasn't exactly the kind of thing you could bother the NYPD with at this point, so she assigned the job to me. I would be her marital TaskRabbit. Nothing about that delegation felt strange to me. If I had a penny for every time a friend said, "You're the only person I can turn to with this. . . ." Well, someone else would be cooking our dinner at a brownstone I actually *owned,* not a third-floor walk-up rental with no dishwasher or laundry that my mother once described as, "Parisian. And mousy."

Suffice to say, within my friends' relationships, I knew where all the bodies were buried.

And though Audra and I didn't know each other so well—Sam and I only moved to the block a few months ago, our first home together!—I assumed she easily intuited that I would not judge. Cheating, infidelity, nonmonogamy, ethical nonmonogamy: I was your woman for all of it. There was nothing I hadn't covered in my "Sex Diaries" column—emotional affairs, sex worker affairs, financial affairs, secret gay affairs, celebrity affairs, etc.—and on a personal level, the safeties and pitfalls of monogamy were some of my favorite things to muse on. Though Sam and I were monogamous in practice, if I had to draw a line in the sand, I still wasn't exactly sure where that line would be.

Would I have an affair? I'd like to believe that if I felt deeply compelled to sleep with someone else that I would be open about it with

Sam, and we would sort it out together—somehow. And vice versa. Maybe we'd open our relationship. Maybe we'd give each other a free pass. I don't know. It hasn't happened yet. And not that there's any correlation, but I'm also very satisfied in ways that—for once— are actually *too personal* to write about. Sam cringes when I hypothesize about any of this, though. He thinks my whole seventies free love shtick is a total sham. To be seen!

As I left Sam and Hazy to fend for themselves and walked over to the town house next door, I was prepared for a tough scene. I didn't think I'd find a cold body or anything, but I assumed Harris would be inconsolable, unrecognizable, and incoherent. He had, in one night, lost everything: his wife, his daughter, his work, his future, his name, his legacy, his money. It's crazy how one bad decision can murder your entire life, and yet, we flawed humans never learn.

When I banged on Harris's door, hoping he was not hanging from the chandelier, I also hoped he would not want to talk-talk about what had happened. Because if he did, I'd probably offer something resembling low-grade sympathy toward him. Was he horrid? Yes! Did I have a soft spot for those who burned everything down in the throes of animalistic desire? Kind of, sometimes. Regardless, I would never break girl code. Whatever his story was, he was now dead to me (if not dead already). A heart-to-heart with her heartless husband is not what Audra was asking for. She simply needed someone to quickly check on him, record that he was alive, and report right back.

I knocked again and again. Nothing.

Suddenly things got real. *Wait.* What if Harris wasn't going to kill himself, but he was going to kill me? I mean, according to Audra, he was a fuckin' sociopath. Or maybe he was the murder-suicide type. I didn't really know this Harris. He seemed quietly cocky in that high-school-tennis-team way, and sort of Scott Peterson–ish. On our occasional run-ins on the block, I noticed he liked Dunkin' Donuts coffee, which flagged me, in the same way it does with Ben Affleck, but that's just an instinct. Being from Massachusetts, I shouldn't be such a DD hater. But, I mean, there were so many more sophisticated, not to mention non-Styrofoam, coffee options around. . . . He could definitely be a monster.

Snooping around the vestibule, I noticed that Audra and Harris OWNED and inhabited all four floors of their home—all four of 'em! That in itself felt like a small betrayal. Was this really worth it? *Is this how I really want to go down?* Sam hadn't legally adopted Hazel yet. We hadn't even told our families that we had begun the filing process. How would anyone know that I explicitly and implicitly wanted him to raise her if I was strangled by the hands of a Dunkies drinker? My parents and sister would all equally want her, and I'd want them to have her too, but not like I wanted her to be with her dad. Hazel's world could erupt into a hideous custody battle! This was not worth it. With more ominous silence at the front door, I thought about firing off an email to my entire address book clearly stating, *IF ANYTHING HAPPENS TO ME, SAM GETS HAZEL.* Emails are legal contracts, right? I also wanted to include the addendum, *AND SHE MUST REMAIN JEWISH!* Oy.

This time, I knocked louder. Harris wasn't answering. Was he seriously bleeding out or what? Did I need to call the police? Then I put my head to the door to see what I could hear, and as I clutched my phone to call Audra or Sam or the FBI, I felt a legitimate wave of extreme worry. Maybe I'd gone too far in the whole marital Task-Rabbit thing. This was not my business. Not my circus, not my monkeys.

Finally I heard some rattling around inside. Then I heard footsteps coming. And suddenly the door swung open and there was Harris. Fresh as a daisy. No slit wrists. No bloodstained goodbye note. Just Dr. Douchebag, drinking a heady IPA, chitchatting with his girlfriend on the phone.

"Hey, you!" he said nearly buoyantly to me. "Sorry. I had to put a shirt on. I thought you were the burrito guy."

Burritos? I was thinking more like fentanyl bottles.

"Uh, nope. No burritos," I replied very cautiously. "I was just checking on you."

Harris told his lovergirl he'd call her right back. Then he came out on the stoop and we sat down together.

According to Harris, he and Audra had been planning to get divorced for several years. She started throwing around the D-bomb right after they got married, like, fifteen years ago. He only started the affair *after* they agreed to basically "fake" their marriage for the sake of their daughter, until she went to college. In other words, according to Harris, this marriage was totally over. So, he met someone else who lit up his life, and he felt free to go for it. There wasn't much guilt involved, for him. As for his work repercussions, the aftermath wasn't nearly as fatalistic as Audra had made it sound.

We've all heard the expression, "There are three sides to every story: yours, mine, and the truth." And I think that's what was happening here. Harris was still a scumbag. And I was Team Audra all the way. But his side of the story was very different from hers. And as the delivery guy came with Harris's burrito, I walked away from the stoop, both relieved and over it. The predominant takeaway, if I'm being honest, was not *I hope they work it out,* but . . . if only they'd participate in my "Both Sides of a Breakup" column. Also, I hoped that turd tipped well.

"Both Sides of a Breakup" was another popular column I sometimes wrote for *NewYork* magazine, though the concept did not originate with me. The way it works is I talk to two exes, separately, about the beginning, middle, and end of their relationship, and then I put the different renditions together as a He Said/She Said (or He Said/He Said . . . They Said/They Said . . . etc.). For example, had Audra and Harris participated in the column, the opening lines might have looked something like this:

Audra: I was sick to my stomach, wondering if he was going to jump off the Brooklyn Bridge or shoot himself in the head.

Harris: It was a very stressful situation. Fatty Daddy Taco had the chunkier guacamole, but Mama Mexicana delivered those frosty micheladas. . . .

Everyone's relationship retellings were always so different. The memories were often conflicting, and the various perspectives were usually quite funny, and sometimes very depressing. The only reason "Both Sides" is not another weekly column for me is because it's impossible to find people to participate. Because, think about it. Let's say I meet someone with a great breakup story. They'd then need to reach out to their ex about talking to me—and most people hate their exes, or they erased their exes' phone numbers a long time ago, or it's way too painful or triggering to try to ever make contact again.

Alternatively, someone can give me their ex's contact information and I'd reach out about interviewing them myself. That's not exactly a slam dunk either. Usually, the exes are like, "Hell no. I'm not touching that! Why would I ever touch that?" Or, "Weird . . . but sure . . . I just can't make time to deal with this until next year, or, ya know, never."

So it's a tricky one to pull off. I wish it weren't, because the exes usually find the exercise to be very cathartic, liberating, and ultimately positive, and I personally find the work quite thought-provoking for myself and the readers.

Convincing ex-couples to take part in the column, however, always does make me feel a little hypocritical, considering I had so much unresolved baggage surrounding pretty much all of my big breakups. Sure, I was evolved enough to find my way to motherhood and Sam, and yet, these relationships still follow me around like dark shadows. I haven't let them go. Every day I try to forget about my exes. And the craziest part is, it's not because I can't bear thinking about them, but I can't bear thinking about *me* with them. Because in my mind, in one way or another, I am still stuck on a not-necessarily-true story that I ruined everything with all of them.

When my ex-fiancé Spike, the Top Chef, recently popped up on my Instragram feed, I surprised myself by taking the plunge and following him. Within a day, he followed me back. And soon, after almost ten years of estrangement, we were back in touch. I scrolled around to see pictures of him and his new wife, which did not make me retch but made me thrilled for him. She seemed sexy and unique and looked like a real force to be reckoned with, and I appreciated all that about her. He needed that. Spike and I DMed with a few little life updates, the names of our kids and partners, and a couple details about work and our parents. After a few innocuous messages—establishing that nothing about our correspondence was shady or suggestive; I did not want to piss off that new wife after all—I felt comfortable enough to ask him, "Why do you think we broke up? Honestly."

As I watched the dot dot dots start and stop again, implying he was crafting and then recrafting his response, I warned myself for what I was about to hear. My negative inner voices were unleashed: That I was too insecure. That nothing could put me out of my misery. That I was an albatross. That all his friends and family hated me for the stress I brought to his world. That I pressured him to have kids when he was still a kid himself. That we could have been perfect, but I poisoned our life.

He wrote: *You were amazing. We were happy. I let my career get in the way.*

What?! His career?! He blamed his freakin' career, in entirety, for our breakup? His career was certainly a challenge, but I'd been blaming my unhinged, unconfident self for all these years. I mean, when I went on my book tour for *Apron Anxiety,* the only city I wouldn't visit was D.C. because I had started so many garbage fires there that I assumed nobody would want me on their turf. And all these years later, Spike thought I was amazing, and we were happy, and it was only his career.

Now. Is there a chance that Spike was just being kind in that DM? Yes. Had he done some work on himself and was practicing the art of accountability? Maybe. Was this his way of not really engaging . . . not poking the beast . . . the beast being me? Perhaps. But if I had to guess, if I had Harris's nonexistent gun to my head, I would say those were genuinely Spike's sentiments. And you know what? I was not going to send them straight to my emotional spam folder just because they sounded too nice to be true. Spike thought that I was amazing and we were happy. Whaddayaknow. His outlook on our time together was so much easier on my heart than mine, so I chose to accept his small gift with graciousness.

The reality is, "Both Sides of a Breakup" is a creative exploration that doesn't make a dent in understanding how or why a relationship decays. If love is the greatest mystery of all, then the death of love is even more inexplicable. We are hardwired to be, at once, fixated on our hearts and completely dumbfounded by what lives inside them. That's just the way it is. No wonder love makes us insane.

Unlocking the details of a bad breakup might help with self-growth or self-compassion, but it won't make saying goodbye, or letting go, any easier. Don't tell Spike's wife, but just DMing him was a whole new heartbreak. And don't tell Sam, but when he's away on work trips, sometimes I slip on my old ruby ring, stare at it longingly, and wish I could rewrite my life.

Closure is for real estate, not love stories.

Nevertheless, you should still consider doing my column.

twenty-three

They Love You, But . . .

Emily in Paris filled me with outrage. Irrational, mismanaged outrage, no doubt. But outrage, nonetheless.

Emily in Paris was one of the many TV shows that I wanted to write for, but I was never hired for the writers' room. And now Emily was not in Paris but in a toxic knot that lived inside the pit of my stomach along with *Togetherness, Modern Love, Love Life,* and *The Affair.* I wanted all of them, but they were all slightly, *just slightly,* out of reach.

My TV agent, Zach, looks like Prince Harry and is a good human being, and I know he cares in a real way about my career. But it is extremely hard to break into TV, as I already knew, and a steadfast agent can only go so far. Throughout the years, every time Zach sent me on meetings to pitch ideas, or simply to endear myself to producers and showrunners, an industry term known as "a general," he would receive and relay the exact same feedback: "They love you, but . . ."

> They love you, but . . . you're a little too green for what
> they're looking for.
> They love you, but . . . the showrunner didn't connect with
> your writing samples.
> They love you, but . . . they need someone whose name
> makes a bigger splash.
> They love you, but . . . the studio has never heard of you.

At the end of all these crushing calls, Zach would always reiterate, "They really did love you, Alyssa."

More love, I did not need. What I needed was to stop being so overlooked and underestimated. And that great Writers Guild health insurance? That sure would've been nice for Hazy and me too.

Several years back I had an excellent meeting with an artsy executive at Charlize Theron's production company, and left feeling extremely positive about my chances to develop something with them. Charlize, after all, was a Single Mom by Choice too—and the main show I was pitching was about a family-run cryobank set in a beachy enclave in Connecticut with a female lead who was as alluring as she was cunning. I called it *Six Feet Under,* with sperm. We could do so much great storytelling together!

A few hours after the meeting in Burbank, one of Zach's colleagues called.

"The producer didn't respond to any of your ideas, but she's obsessed with you, and wants to be your best friend. She literally said 'I want to be her BFF.'"

"I was there for over an hour! She didn't like *anything* I said?"

"Nothing in terms of work, no. But she really wants to hang out. Can I give her your cell?"

Another BFF I did not need either.

There were countless versions of that story, and they all made me mad. Why didn't I try to break in when I was younger, and less . . . desperate? Why didn't my mother push me to move to LA and intern for some big shot on *Friends* the way she pushed me to never wear pants to shul, or get my thyroid checked at my yearly, or handwrite all my thank-yous? No one in my family pressured me to be anything but myself and I resented them for that!

Maybe I just sucked at TV writing and it was easier telling me I was too green than too crap. But why would a high-level agent like Zach invest in me if there was no hope at all? And why would these famous, award-winning producers read my work and make time for these "generals" if I was entirely without promise? No one was doing it just to be nice—because no one in Hollywood is actually nice. There had to be something there. I just had to unlock the right door. Until then, for every TV series I didn't get, I shape-shifted and told myself it was more time to spend with my daughter. For every season of *The Mindy Project* I lost out on, that was another year of the Hazel project that I was 100 percent there for. That was very hard to argue with. Although, because I loved my kid so much, I also wanted to make money for her future!

It didn't help that around the time I turned forty, I realized that many of my friends had gotten rich. It wasn't surprising, per se. They were all intelligent and ambitious, and had the Privilege (capital *P*) of a good education and terrific opportunities; they all worked hard, never slept, and were willing and able to destroy anyone who got in their way. With brains, beauty, connections, cajones, fangs, and in some cases, powerful fathers—these young ballers had all of it.

While I was spending my days bullshitting about umami, my friend Jay was an early investor in Uber. While I was swirling wine that tasted like "Swedish Fish having sex in a tobacco field," Shelley— whose life motto was "You say 'no' and I hear 'maybe'"—was convincing Amazon that she should handle their public relations. Like, all of it. The girls I partied with in my twenties now owned global marketing firms with multimillion-dollar clients like Honest and goop. The Wall Street peons I dated, who were so anxious about their Christmas bonuses that they couldn't get it up, now made *fuck-you money* at their own hedge funds. The exhausted, miserable law school students now repped world leaders and regularly appeared on *Good Morning America*. The eccentric DIY gal I once shared a walk-up apartment with became a booming Walmart brand. The hot, chatty guy who once bought me a whiskey sour and was just starting his first grown-up job now runs Plan B production company with Brad Pitt (and *also* never hired me for a writers' room). The earnest sports fan sold his earnest sports blog and now sails around the world on a yacht. A big-swingin'-dick food writer who started an elite restaurant app sold it to AMEX, and then bought Liv Tyler's town house and Betsey Johnson's beach house. My scrappy and happy spin instructors sprouted into a little thing called SoulCycle. And a handful of awkward, unglamorous writer friends converted their books into films, and their films into sequels, and their sequels into trust funds for their children and their children's children and so on.

Me? I had a column about New Yorkers schtupping each other. I wrote a charming little book that went nowhere fast. Sometimes I landed cushy assignments about breakups or Botox or being a perfectly imperfect mom—but those I could write in my sleep (and with a young child, I sometimes did). Sure, I was constantly sent free s'mores kits and CBD bath salts and lingerie subscriptions and samples of Mary J. Blige's wine line, with hopes that I'd include them in my next "Best Valentine's Day Gifts" roundup or the like, but all that did was solidify me as the friend you always invited to a dinner party because I brought the bomb-ass swag.

My career was okay. It would be wrong to complain. I hadn't paid for a "pleasure serum" or a protein bar in fifteen years. Daily Harvest sent me free "Forager Bowls"! As the Jews say, "Dayenu!" But when I compared my accomplishments to those of everyone else I'd come up with in New York, to me, there wasn't much to look at. While they were quantifiable successes, I was still such a striver. We live in a culture where self-worth and net worth are very close friends, and though I lean toward the side of down-to-earth, I have never been desensitized to any of that.

On a crisp fall day, I had a coffee with my sister at Cobble Hill Park, a sweet little spot between both of our apartments. Rachel was wearing a beautiful camel peacoat, mom jeans, and dad sneakers. She had just given birth to Phoebe, my darling baby niece. Hazel and my nephew, Charles, were both three years old and off doing cultural things with our parents, and by cultural things I mean getting hot dogs at Costco. I had just come off of weeks of finagling for a spot in the *Sweetbitter* writers' room. *Sweetbitter* was a fabulous book about restaurant life written by the formidable Stephanie Danler, and the TV version, coming out on Starz, was meant to be just as cool and contemplative as her original pages. In my mind, I was destined for that writers' room. Not only was it filmed in New York, which is rare, but most of my thirties revolved around the seductive world of chefdom and restaurant people. Every word of my memoir was about finding belonging in that odd and intoxicating subculture. I had so many stories to mine, so much emotional currency to offer.

A few minutes before I sat down with Rachel in the park, however, I received the final hard pass from Zach.

He read me the email that just came in.

I love Alyssa, but . . . she's just not right for this season. It was from the showrunner, whom I kind of knew socially, thus it cut even worse.

"I'm really sorry," Zach said on the phone upon hearing my heart sink.

"All good. Thanks for trying." I sighed.

A few weeks earlier, I had asked the showrunner to have breakfast with me at a little French spot in the West Village, where I all but begged him to hire me for the writers' room. He couldn't have been more gracious with his time and advice, but when I swallowed my pride and told him, point-blank, how badly I needed to catch a break, he encouraged me to "work through it" in my material. The subtext being, stop whining and start writing. The sub-subtext being, the *Sweetbitter* set was no place for me to pitch my tent.

"What happened?" Rach asked at the park, sensing my despair.

The only words I had were: "I don't want to die a wasted talent."

Rach, who had no idea what I was talking about, looked befuddled.

"Are you dying?"

"My dreams are. But no. God forbid. I'm fine."

I tried to find the words.

"You know the whole, 'Try again. Fail again. Fail better' thing? Well, fuck that! Let someone with a Netflix deal fail better. Let the Duplass brothers fail better. My failures, as I get older, just hurt worse and worse. My career never went anywhere exciting, and I know it could have, and that's the hard part! I know I could have been successful. Like, *Fleabag* successful! Well, not *Fleabag* successful. She's freakin' brilliant. The point is, I can't seem to make any forward progress no matter how hard I try."

"But, Lys!" she said, her big chestnut-brown eyes now penetrating mine. "You *are* successful!"

I didn't want to hear that. I was forty-two years old. I didn't have enough savings to buy a small house anywhere, even in rural Maine. My supremely generous and caring friend Danyelle Freeman and her husband, Josh, paid for Hazel's first year of preschool, which they insisted on, and I let them. Sure, I had Sam now, and while he was a busy and in-demand filmmaker, it's hard to strike gold in documentaries. And that was beside the point.

"You've always achieved your goals," Rach continued. "You wanted to write for *The New York Times* since you were two years old and now you write for *The New York Times*!"

"One article," I reminded her. "And another in the works. But go on . . ."

"You wanted a baby, but not a husband, so you made a baby without a husband. I mean, that's something most women would find impossible to do. Which reminds me, you have a toddler! And no childcare besides Mom and Dad. Maybe it's time to cut yourself some slack . . . give yourself a little break?"

One look from me and she knew that was the incorrect answer.

"Okay. Let me try this. You are literally capable of the impossible, Lys. So let's figure out the exact goal here. Name it. Because once you name it, you will get it."

"I want to prove to myself, and everyone else, that I can get my own show."

"Then do it!" she cheered. "Whatever it takes, do it! I will help any way I can."

We looked at each other, sufficiently inspired, and wrapped up the chat to pick up our favorite productions, our kiddos.

Over the next year, I made it my mission to achieve this goal at any cost. Dog, meet bone. Zach and I went hard. I flew myself to LA and back every few weeks, with Sam and my family juggling Hazel's preschool drop-offs, ballet lessons, and playdates. Zach set up dozens and dozens of meetings for me. Reese Witherspoon's people. Lorne Michaels's people. Kaley Cuoco's people. Margot Robbie's people. Ben Stiller's people. Adam Sandler's people. Mila Kunis's people. Chelsea Handler's people. With blazing confidence, I marched myself right into any door that was even slightly ajar, flung myself into their tulip chairs, and tried to make them believe that I was a bankable human writer and I wanted a seat at the table.

Bullishly, I pitched and pitched and pitched. There was never a moment when I wasn't extreme working or extreme mothering. I

rescheduled a routine mammogram nine times. Nine times! I bla-
tantly *skipped* one of my best friend's weddings because I felt like
death after a red-eye, and had a toddler with pink eye. I owed all
my loved ones phone calls, email responses, and belated birthday
texts; I took on no other work besides the "Sex Diaries" column.
None. Everything I had went to one goal and one goal only: landing
that show.

And yet. After 365 days of shuffling around my kid, deprioritiz-
ing my relationship, and pushing forward like a maniac with insuf-
ficient travel miles, the feedback from the Hollywood gatekeepers
largely remained: *They. Love.You. But.*

On an unusually cool day in LA—black leather jacket weather—I
got very sick before heading to Sony studios. I had one last hope
for a series. It was called *New Love City,* and it was about two sexy
and complex female matchmakers trying to find love for New York's
most interesting and offbeat characters. I didn't have much steam
left for yet another round of bloodsucking pitches, but I loved the
producer attached to the series—Alison Greenspan from Doug
Robinson Productions—and would have worked on any project, in
any industry, just to collaborate with her. Alison had a reputation
for being incredibly supportive of women, and fiercely loyal to the
people she cared about. Whereas everyone else in Hollywood had
made me feel slightly defective, Alison made me feel like I could do
no wrong. As beat-down as I was, because she still believed in me, I
still believed in me.

But there was no way I could make it to Sony in this condition.
My head was splitting. My stomach was sour. I kept gagging, as if I
were going to throw up. The closest CVS was half a mile from my

hotel and as I carted myself there, I had to take hold of a dirty West Hollywood traffic light so as to not fall down or pass out. The headache and nausea were so extreme that I decided to find a pharmacist once I got there and ask if he had any prescription migraine medicine. Though I'd never had a migraine before, I assumed that's what this was. *What else could it be?*

As I waited my turn in line to approach the counter, I sat on the grimy CVS rug with my head buried in my hands, clutching my tote that read *Wake up. Kick Ass. Repeat,* in case the vomit erupted and I needed a receptacle to catch it.

It was finally my turn. As I slowly stood up in the swaying pharmacy, my eyes caught a glimpse of something behind the counter. And just like you might see in a rom-com—not written by me, goddamn it—I blinked. I blinked hard.

It was a pregnancy test.

And that's when I realized that this was not a migraine. This was morning sickness.

twenty-four

Sex Diaries: The Docuseries

At forty-two years old and eight months pregnant, I had one last question for the big, bad world: "Is cheesecake ice cream a thing?"

I thought it was a thing. I could have sworn I saw it somewhere aspirational, like a Van Leeuwen. But I definitely might have just dreamed about it. My dreams were so vivid that sometimes it was hard to distinguish what happened in real life from what happened in dream life. Once, in college, I dreamed about kissing a random French kid I went to sleepaway camp with years back. The kiss felt so real, and it was so luscious, that when I woke up, I had no other choice but to take my emergency money and follow the feeling to Paris. There, we fell madly in love. We dated for two transcontinental years only to break up when he spent a summer in New York and revealed a shopping addiction that verged on severe mental illness.

As I studiously surfed the internet for my cheesecake ice cream answers—don't give me any of that vegan shit—an email appeared that turned out to be a different spoonful of magic.

Hi, Alyssa, my name is Jenny Carchman and I am a documentary film-maker based in NYC. I'm writing because I am developing a series based on "Sex Diaries" and was told you are the "Sex Diaries" columnist for the magazine. I am wondering if you'd be free for a coffee. . . .

I screamed for Sam.

"Have you ever heard of Jenny Carchman?"

"Yes," he said. "Why?"

He went on to say that Jenny was a very well-respected film-maker and that if this was something she was developing, it was likely a very legitimate project. He assumed the series was also in conjunction with HBO because everyone knew they were big fans of hers. Then I forwarded Jenny's email to my agent, took a screenshot to show my parents and sister, and after waiting an available-but-not-too-available hour and a half to respond, I wrote Jenny back.

I told her that I was indeed the writer of the column, that I'd been writing it for six years. Also, I wanted her to know that I was savvy in TV development—too savvy, in fact, as *New Love City,* the matchmaking series, had just been rejected by NBC at the eleventh hour. *And* that my baby daddy worked in documentaries too. In closing, I made sure to clearly communicate: *Yes, yes, yes, please, please, please, please. Please let me be part of this docuseries or else I will seriously lose it.* Speaking of, I also alerted Jenny to the fact that I was pushing out a little boy in the next few weeks, and was at risk of that life-threatening preeclampsia again, but we could easily work around all of that.

A few days later, Jenny and I met for a coffee near our apartments, a mere ten minutes from each other. She confirmed that the series *was* in the works over at HBO and I hopefully confirmed to her that I was important to the project. Soon after that, everyone (yas queen, including me!) was drafting contracts with their various agents and entertainment lawyers, and the team started thinking about how to make the thing come to life. Jenny was a visionary and a leader and there was such great synergy. The deal was almost done. There were just a few loose ends. The most critical loose end being that I had to meet with HBO. They wanted us all in the same room for a preliminary brainstorm session.

As we started to throw out dates, I went into labor.

Just like with Hazel, it was another dramatic childbirth threatened by preeclampsia. We knew that might happen and yet we weren't at all prepared. Sam was filming a series in Ohio and had to abandon ship in the middle of the gig, handing his camera gear over to a complete stranger so he could get to New York by hell or high water. A new friend from my building, Sara—whose last name I didn't even know yet—made it over twenty seconds after I called her to babysit Hazel, until my sister ran, full speed, from her apartment to mine to take over. Sam's parents, Jeje and Pops, were just landing in New York from Maine, and somehow remained calm and high-functioning through all of this, bless them. My parents rushed to NYU via Uber—the only time they'd ever forgo public transportation—and mind you, it killed them, it fucking killed them.

Who knows why but I was set on having a VBAC—vaginal birth after Cesarean. So, that was fun. I tore six ways till Sunday and threw up all over Sam, who made it to NYU just in time to hear the unspeakable sounds coming from my . . . ugh, let's not even talk about it. I wailed until my throat was raw, howling over and over, "How do people do this without drugs?" The doctors and nurses were exceptional and patient, even though I had no idea what I was supposed to do. Why I had googled both Tinsley Mortimer's and Luann de Lesseps's mug shots several dozen times, but never read one single word on how to extract a baby from my vagina, I will never understand about myself. After just enough agony that I truly got the point, Sam and I had a nine-pound bundle of joy.

River Jewett Russell was here. River Jewett Russell, aka Mordechai Sholom, aka Tony Potato, aka Esteban the Magnificent, aka the Senator, aka Shmutzy Mutzy, aka Big Riv. We named him after Sam's wonderful grandfather, Ralph Jewett, who would die a few days later, that November. I like to think that his spirit was passed on to our gorgeous son.

Being that River was a Russell, he was perfect. He slept beautifully. He nursed beautifully. He grew beautifully. If Hazel was my miracle baby, River was my angel baby. We all adored him, and the best part of all was that Hazy had a brother. She would have him by her side for the rest of her life. She would never be alone after Sam and I left the earth, and that's all I needed to know—especially, once again, when faced with my own mortality.

The preeclampsia kept me quite sick in the hospital for an extra few days, with River and Sam by my side so that I could breastfeed despite all the wires, tubes, and needles stuck into my body. When I fought to leave because I couldn't take it anymore, I had to sign some paperwork that I was exiting against doctors' orders. It was very risky, but I had to get home to Hazel. I missed her too much, arguing that my yearning for my daughter was going to kill me before the blood pressure. I missed her chipped front tooth, her ravishing honey-colored hair tickling my face, how she called the remote "the temote" and Nutella "mutella" and rocks "cocks" (couldn't make that one up!). I missed her stuffie, a bedraggled pig named Mimi from IKEA, who we converted to Judaism, hence her full name, Miriam Rivka. I missed my darling little Hazy-bear, who never left the house without her rainbow purse, glittery eye shadow palette, or pink gum. Though Hazel is not allowed to use this word, I *hated* being away from her.

And—okay, fine—I wanted to get home to HBO, too. We still had to schedule that meeting. So after a night of rest back at our apartment, now an NYU outlaw, I checked in with the team. I couldn't sit, walk, pee, or poop without screaming bloody murder, but I also could not let this show go on without me. We set the meeting. I would be three weeks postpartum. It was going to be at the HBO offices up at the Hudson Yards, that super-modern mega-complex described in *New York* magazine as a "billionaire's fantasy city."

Hudson Yards was also about an hour-and-a-half trek from my apartment in Brooklyn, which in lactation time meant: uh-oh. The plan was to pump on the A train on the way there, and then pump again on my way back. If anybody had a problem with it, I'd *dare* them to say something.

On the day of the meeting, I was extremely sleep-deprived and the house was pure pandemonium. There's a quote that goes something like, "One kid is one kid, two kids is twenty kids" and goodness, is it true. I didn't have time to shower or put makeup on, and the only thing that fit was an oversized Alexander Wang sweater with huge rhinestones all over the sleeves, which sort of made me look like a mob wife on her way to a Weight Watchers meeting, but also like a *Project Runway* contestant named Tatiana. When I sat on the subway, not that I could sit without immense shooting pain or ripping a stitch, I realized that I'd forgotten to pack the breast pump.

At this point, all I could do was pray that my boobs, already enlarged, but not yet engorged, would cooperate. As for my face, when I got to Hudson Yards, I had about fifteen minutes to fix myself up. As the HBO headquarters are connected to a luxury mall, I fortuitously found a Sephora. There, I smacked a blush in the shade of "Quickie" all over my face. I rubbed a dark red lipstick called "Vendetta" on my mouth and sprayed myself with a perfume labeled "Florgasm." The one thing I actually needed, two dabs of under-eye concealer, completely escaped me.

When I checked in at HBO, all boobies and rouge, I was surprised not to see anyone else associated with the project in the lobby. Stella Bugbee, the editor in chief of "The Cut" (at the time) and a New York City fashion icon, was supposed to be there, as were some of the magazine's other influential names. But no one was around. It was just me and a handsome gentleman named Chad— who looked exactly . . . I mean *exactly* . . . like Bradley Cooper— and who was SVP of Entertainment at Vox (which owns *New York* magazine). Which is to say, Chad was the Boss Man.

Chad curiously phoned his assistant. *Where is everyone?* Turns out there had been a technical glitch and I was the only one who received the meeting invitation. *Oof.* This was the do-or-die meeting with HBO and all he had to show for it was a hot mess on the brink of mastitis who was having a Florgasm.

On the elevator ride up to the meeting, I wondered if Chad was as worried as I was about being stuck with me as his wingperson. It had been weeks since I'd formed a complete sentence other than, "How bad does your butt have to itch before you know it's a hemorrhoid?" I wanted Stella and the gang there badly, and I'm sure he did too!

We were escorted to the conference room. Before the HBO executives joined us, I excused myself to go to the bathroom, where I tried to hand-express my own nipples, cupping my breasts and squeezing them into oblivion. It did the trick. Then I looked at myself in the mirror. Of all my Rachel Comey jumpsuits and badass bomber jackets and microdermabrasions and midnight-blue eyeliners, here I was, for the meeting of a lifetime, a complete and utter clown. I had to laugh to keep from crying. Then I had to get back to the conference room.

By some miracle, the meeting went swimmingly. The women who ran HBO's unscripted department were overwhelmingly warm, funny, and smart. They kept asking me questions about the column. I wanted to sound sophisticated and cool and dazzle the room like Stella Bugbee might have; however, in my compromised state, I could only be so captivating.

"Hopefully I can answer all your questions articulately," I said. "But I had a baby three weeks ago, so I'm a little off my game."

The executives appeared to be flabbergasted by this information. "You had a baby *three* weeks ago?"

"Yeah, my son, River. He's my second child. I had my daughter on my own, with a sperm donor, four years ago. This one, I made the old-fashioned way . . . from sex . . . with a real live penis. So *retro, right*? I mean . . . what I'm trying to say is . . . Yes. I just had a baby with my partner, Sam."

"Tell us more!" beamed one executive.

"Actually, tell us everything!" urged the other.

I looked over at Chad. He nodded enthusiastically, like, *Go, sis! Go!*

So I presented HBO with the whole story. The engagements, the heartbreaks, Rome, the fibroids, Dr. Grifo, Vince Vaughn, and Verona Island. Hormonal, and well, human, I got emotional talking so intimately about my journey. My stories were not witty or provocative, they were real and they were raw. And you know what else was raw? My . . . as Hazel would say . . . "Private." And so I told them about that, too. And just when it was time to shift gears and get into the mechanics of the series, I said I had to leave because my tits were exploding and my baby needed me. There was a chance I blew the whole thing by ending the meeting so abruptly, but I had to respect my body. And HBO *definitely* respected that.

As we got up to say goodbye, the more senior executive said, "You have to be in this show, Alyssa! We should film you doing your job. Would you be open to that?" Gobsmacked, I looked at her like I must have misunderstood. Of everything I have ever written, there is no more factual sentence than the following: I never looked so terrible in my entire life. I am not being self-deprecating. My outfit was all wrong. I was thirty pounds over my regular weight. There was nothing chic about me other than the bucket bags under my eyes. And, yeah, I guess there's something poignant about being genuinely liked and respected when I was so uncharacteristically stripped down. But still: holy shit, what?!

Of course no one really knew if I'd be "on" the show or how any of it would coalesce creatively, and frankly the idea of being on camera didn't particularly matter to me one way or another.

However, the meeting set the table for a spectacular turn of events in my career and my confidence. I was finally an intrinsic part of a TV series, and it felt 100 percent validating, gratifying, and great.

As I descended back down to earth and toward the lobby of the HBO building, I glided into the elevator chamber, adjusted my undergarments, and screamed.

twenty-five

Smitty

I get kicked out of things all the time.

Some Yahoo mom group kicked me out when I called a notoriously rude shop owner "a witch" because I thought it would be wrong to call her "a bitch." It offended someone from the Wicca community and I feel bad about that, and learned from it.

Facebook kicked me out—or at least tried to—when I innocuously commented that I wanted to "kidnap" my friend Elissa's new baby because he was so damn cute. The Facebook police said, and I quote, "Your comment goes against our community standards on violence and incitement." *Yikes!*

The writerly coffee shop down the street from my apartment regularly kicks me out for working there without ordering anything—which, guilty as charged, but I'm not a fan of their coffee beans, so tell me, what am I supposed to do? I always leave a good tip on my way out.

Even as I wrote this book, my building (my own building!) kicked me out of ALL AMENITIES, not once but TWICE, because I kept getting busted for snacking on our communal roof, where food was not allowed due to COVID protocol. Both times, I was completely alone, vaccinated, and legit starving—and also, I am a burned-out, stressed-out working mom who enjoys a sweet potato chip, *but okay*. Poor judgment.

The one place I never thought I'd get kicked out of? High school. And yet, six minutes after my tongue touched alcohol for the first time, I got suspended from Longmeadow High.

It was the evening of the variety show, freshman year, and all my preppy friends were singing a bad rendition of "Paradise by the Dashboard Light," which felt way too corny for a cool cat like me. Other things I just couldn't get down with while growing up in Massachusetts included J. Crew roll-neck sweaters, those ugly shoes called bucks, field hockey, ski club, sailing camp, Nantucket red, mayonnaise, jambands, and Catholic guilt. As the token Jew within the popular group, I came to identify as a young "individualist" and I did not mind it at all. At the end of the day, we were all a bunch of dirty-minded Massholes anyway. And that night, the only thing that set me apart from my friends was that I was a dirty-minded Masshole *not* pretending to be Meat Loaf.

I stood in the back of the auditorium, unamused. My itchy purple vintage dress from Northampton (heaven, to teenage me) was ill-fitting and stiff, but it was still better than all the fleece around me. I couldn't even with the Patagonia. I was getting restless waiting for the show to end, counting down to the thing we did every Friday night: follow cute boys in their parents' Jeeps into scary swamplands filled with snakes and pervs, with the hopes that someone would take us to first, second, sloppy-second, third, or sloppy-third base.

While digging under my polyester gown to scratch under my bra, two girlfriends from another circle tapped me on the shoulder.

"Wanna come drink with us?" said one of them into my ear.

"Where?" I whispered back.

"Cafeteria bathroom," mouthed the other girl.

Hmmm. Did I want to get drunk inside a pungent, pee-splattered bathroom stall? It wasn't exactly the thing my high school dreams were made of. In fact, I'd never drank before. My parents didn't drink, so I never so much as had a sip of champagne at a wedding or a taste of Manischewitz at a Passover seder. But I was fifteen years old and curious, and my other friends were still "cold and lonely in the deep dark night." It had to happen at some point, so why not now?

We went to the bathroom and squatted around a filthy toilet seat and passed around some stolen gin. It tasted sharp and horrible, but the tingle of rebellion was tasty, and I liked it. Before I could even check in with my brain to see if I had a buzz on—*whatever a buzz even was*—the bathroom doors slammed open, and there was the principal, Dr. Murphy. We were busted. Someone ratted us out. Dr. Murphy took us to his office and called our parents. They were all at their respective New England-y dinner parties, except for mine, who were at a Shabbat dinner that definitely did *not* involve Ritz Crackers, bacon bits, or dirty martinis. Our parents had to come take us home immediately. So, instead of kicking it with the boys' varsity lacrosse team, I got temporarily kicked out of school.

We all had to stay home for a week. My mother was usually not strict at all, but since her father had struggled with alcoholism, this was the worst thing that one of her kids could have done. There was no gray area: my mother did not want us drinking. She was extremely upset. And I was grounded indefinitely. My mom was my best friend and I felt like shit for triggering her with the booze. That was the worst punishment of all.

Once I was back at school, Dr. Murphy said I had to attend an after-school rehab program with the other girls a few days a week for an entire month. It was more like detention with Diet Coke, but I still felt like Drew Barrymore talking about it. Obviously, for the sake of being provocative, I was hoping for more of an intervention-type program, but then again, I'd never even been drunk or high before. Fake rehab, however, did offer one thing that felt quite restorative: an exquisite collection of Longmeadow High School's finest, baddest boys.

The bad boys would cruise into fake rehab casually, in between football practice, sessions with their bands, and having sex with their pretty girlfriends who could all leave their houses with wet hair that smelled like Salon Selectives without ever worrying about frizz. The most adorable troublemaker of all was a guy named Matt Smith, who everyone called "Smitty." (Remember: Massholes.) Smitty had long, brown, wavy hair, a sweet soul, a cool Saab, and cystic fibrosis. Rumor had it, Smitty was about to outlive his life expectancy, which was nineteen or something unbelievably young like that. I loved him instantly not only for his luscious teenage babe-ness—he was *the* definition of "wicked fahkin' hot"—but because I knew he was a miracle in a man bun. Young Ethan Hawke could have totally played him in a movie *and* won an Independent Spirit Award for it.

Smitty was nice to me. He paid attention to me. Our friendship felt like something I stole from the back of a truck. Because he was sophisticated in the "creative kid from an intellectual, blended family whose lives did not revolve around Longmeadow" kind of way, I think he picked up on the fact that we were both destined for bigger things, to get out of town, to *live*. Maybe he even sensed my future New York writer vibe, which most of my classmates couldn't quite grasp, even though I always knew that's who I was.

Our mothers were only distant acquaintances, but they were fond of each other. That made me feel even closer to Smitty. My mom didn't fit in with the average suburban housewife, not that she wanted to. She was Jewy and zany, in her bohemian-by-way-of-Marshalls outfits and open-minded perspectives on life. She was remarkably comfortable with herself and had no interest in keeping up with the Joneses. Nor would she ever play golf at the Longmeadow Country Club, where a lot of the ladies convened. Unless they were prestigious doctors—and we were hardly prestigious doctors—Jews weren't wanted there anyway or so it seemed.

For the next few years of high school, Smitty was my big, bad crush, but we were also good pals. He had a long-term girlfriend who liked to hike and listen to Phish, and was gorgeous without a stitch of makeup, and I never stood a chance next to her. We never even came close to hooking up. I did (often) flash all his friends when I finally learned how to get drunk properly, but I am almost positive that Smitty, respectfully, looked away.

After high school, he trekked off to an earthy-crunchy college

somewhere out West, to study biology, which blossomed into orni-
thology and zoology, and I went straight to New York to write and
get weird. My family followed me straight to the Upper West Side,
and we've all been city folk since.

Thirteen years after high school, when Smitty and I were both
around thirty years old, I friended him on Facebook with a little
note. First and foremost, I wanted to hear that he was healthy and
doing well and, likely, I was in between boyfriends and felt like
dangling a carrot his way just in case. Within a few hours he wrote
back:

> Hi, It's so nice to hear from you! I think of you too, and
> figured that I'd never run into you again—but of course,
> who would have predicted Facebook. . . .
>
> Things are good here. I'm in the middle of my PhD
> in zoology. I study horseshoe crab reproductive behav-
> ior, which forces me to do all of my research out on the
> beach. My girlfriend just started here, so I'll be in Florida
> for a few more years, and then hopefully find a nice pro-
> fessorship somewhere.
>
> I've heard various disjunct tales of your success,
> something about writing for magazines . . . you'll have to
> fill me in on the real deal. What is your book about—all
> the crazy shit you did in high school?
>
> Well, I hope all is well, and it sounds like your life is
> going nicely. Perhaps, we'll run into each other back in
> MA one day.
>
> —Matt

How I loved getting a letter from him, even with the overt "girl-friend" hint.

After that, I started following Matt's life online, sometimes opening Facebook just to see what he was up to. Subconsciously, I think I wanted to content myself by checking that he was still in good health, for at least that day.

In 2019, and now in our forties, Matt documented a double lung transplant, sharing every detail of the stupendous journey along the way. He wanted all his friends and family to know what he was going through, generously describing the ultra-complicated procedures in layman's terms, and assuring us he was fighting with all his might to stay strong. He looked as handsome as ever, but was increasingly pale and thin. Everyone I knew from my hometown was praying for him. All in all, the transplant was a groundbreaking success, and Smitty lived—happily—to enjoy his new, kick-ass breathers. Near and far, friends cheered him on the road to complete recovery. If there were ever a reason not to hate on social media, it was the collective support for this beautiful man on this terrifying journey.

Around the time Smitty got his new lungs, I gave birth to River. Thinking about the kind of young man I hoped River would be, more than once, I daydreamed, *Wouldn't it be cool if he was somethin' like Smitty. . . .*

Then, when River was a few months old, the coronavirus hit. We quickly made our way to Maine to spend the next several months with Sam's family, and while we were settling in, I stopped going on Facebook so much. Riding out the worst days of the pandemic on a farm with the Russells was a godsend—especially with Jeje and Pops's generous demeanor and excellent taste in Netflix series and

Argentinian red wine—but it was still a nonstop avalanche of stress for everyone, everywhere.

The "Sex Diaries" column became increasingly precarious to write while New York was under lockdown. I didn't want to feature irresponsible people doing irresponsible things—but I also needed to find sex-related stories each week if I wanted to get paid. Every diary entry posed an ethical dilemma. For example, I was introduced to a self-proclaimed nymphomaniac who said she was still having casual sex with strangers, *but* with her mask on. That left me with quite the moral quandary. Ultimately, I did not do a diary with her. Another potential diarist sent in an entire week's journal, which was juicy enough, until it ended with him in his garage polishing off his HANDGUN. Yeah, no.

As for the *Sex Diaries* docuseries, just as filming was underway, life as we knew it stopped. Now that we lived in a world where single people could no longer meet up for a spicy fish taco, let alone to screw on a sun-drenched daybed, production was somewhat in purgatory. Not to say there was no work to be done. Zoom after Zoom, we tried to figure out next steps, new cast members, and how to plan ahead, knowing it could be years before people connected intimately in any recognizable way.

As such, with a baby, a kindergartener in remote learning, a new book deal (hi!), my columns, the TV stuff, and the constant worrying about our families' health, and the hurt of human beings everywhere, I did not have a spare second to do anything but work and mother for a good twelve months. Not to mention, politically speaking, the world was on fire—and those tensions and divisions were felt deeply and disturbingly in Maine. A socially distanced trip to the grocery store meant dodging jacked-up trucks with MAGA flags, and combative shoppers who refused to wear masks.

It was an awful year, and like all working moms, I was run ragged. My nerves were shot. Something as simple as "More juice please" would make me want to throw things and break things. As for the state of my relationship with Sam, let's just say that I was so touched-out and freaked-out that I penned a story for *The New York Times* declaring that for parents, SEX IS DEAD. The story went viral.

One day, however, I did find some time to lie around in bed with my laptop and peruse Facebook. The kids were with Jeje and Pops at the Farm. We had moved into a rental house not far away from them, and I had a rare quiet moment to myself. The first status update I saw was from Smitty. *Oh good,* I thought. *What a nice distraction!* As my eyes narrowed in on the update, though, I realized it was actually an update from Matt's mom, Margie, posted on his page. *Oh no.*

> It is with a heavy heart that I share with you all the sad news of the passing of my beloved son, Matt Smith, earlier today. . . .

I couldn't read past *my beloved son.*

And when I did, I curled up in a ball and wailed. The coronavirus had me in such a frenzied state that I had forgotten about Smitty's lungs. COVID-19 was a deadly respiratory illness. *How could I have forgotten to check on Smitty's lungs?*

As it turned out, the coronavirus didn't get him, but it didn't help him either. To vastly oversimplify it, Matt died from a series of unexpected complications following the transplant. His last days alive were in the palliative unit of a Boston hospital during COVID, preparing, as much as one can, to die comfortably, with dignity, and with profound inner peace. He had limited visitors, but he willed himself to live long enough to say goodbye to those he loved most, some of whom traveled across the country in the pandemic just to hold him, and listen to music together, until the end.

On the day Smitty took his last breath, his mom was on the way to the hospital. As she drove over the bridge that led to the parking lot, she knew in her heart that he was dying at that very moment. Due to COVID protocol, the security guards would not let her upstairs as she stood there pleading, "But my son is dying; my son is dying. . . ." By the time the nurse came down to retrieve her, he was gone.

We all knew Matt Smith would die young. His doctors—who adored him, not only for his cognizance of science but also for his mindfulness of the human experience—knew he would face death earlier than most. His mother hoped she was wrong, but she, too, was painfully aware he would likely die in her lifetime. Matt himself knew that his life was finite in a way that his friends' lives were not, and for that reason he was deliberate in living as creatively, passionately, and abundantly as possible. God had a plan and everyone was looped in. And yet, his death felt overwhelmingly senseless— especially during this pandemic. All I could think was: *Why do all these maskless assholes with perfect lungs get to live long, nice lives, to be a hundred years old, to know their kids and grandkids, and this Sweet Angel of a Bird Nerd and Bad Boy had to leave the earth before any of them?*

Life is cruel. But I know Matt would have corrected me here to say that life is also good. And then maybe, he would have played me one of his favorite songs by the Avett Brothers, "No Hard Feelings."

When my body won't hold me anymore
And it finally lets me free
Will I be ready?

Matt lived twenty-five years longer than some people predicted, and he made those years count in love, laughter, ladybugs, dragonflies, and dreams. Nevertheless, as the news of Smitty's death sank in, I could not stop crying. And it lasted, on and off, for weeks, mostly when my kids weren't watching. When they *were* watching, I'd tell Hazel that they were happy tears, because I loved her and River and Sam so much it hurt, to which she insisted that we commemorate said happy tears with a Happy Meal. She definitely scored a few McNuggets off my mourning, but that's okay.

Magical thinking helped with the sadness. Throughout the summer, I often looked up at the sky and watched the clouds pass, while visualizing Smitty and Anthony Bourdain filming an episode of *No Reservations* up in heaven. I saw them drinking cold beer and eating street meat somewhere off the beaten path, somewhere they probably weren't supposed to be, way away from heaven's gate; Smitty would be enlightening Bourdain with the fact that horseshoe crabs are not actually crabs at all, and Bourdain would be toasting to Smitty's radically punk lung history. The scene was so vivid in my mind, I could taste the kabobs and see their bare, tanned feet. Cameras rolling. Hearts breaking. The world breathless from their grit and greatness.

And maybe something like that is really happening up above. Why not imagine that we all go on to live in *Parts Unknown* together? If we find out we're wrong when the time comes, who cares? We'll be dead. *With no hard feelings.*

The truth is, I can't remember if Matt Smith was a snowboarder or a food snob or a cat lover or a libertarian; he wasn't my one true love, or my very best friend. I don't want to be a grief thief here. All I know for sure is that Matt Smith might have been born with a life-threatening disease, but he was also born with a devastating amount of soul, and those of us who knew him were blessed to have had him.

A lot of girls would chase Smitty throughout his lifetime. I only hope he knew that we'd chase him long after his death too.

twenty-six

My Wedding Dress

When Hazel turned five years old, she announced she wanted to be a fashion designer.

Prior to that revelation, she wanted to be a babysitter, a "cooker," Taylor Swift, and a spa lady. The newfound fashionista dream, however, appeared to have more lasting power than any of them, as it was fiercely endorsed and mentored by her older cousin Rosie, who never met a crop top she didn't love, and who, at nine years old, was very cosmopolitan and knew how to sew.

One winter night in Maine, with all the Russell siblings and grandparents gathered at the Farm, Hazel and Rosie announced to the family that they were launching a capsule collection. And that the first piece from their cousin collaboration was going to be . . . roll out the red carpet . . . "a wedding dress for Alyssa!"

All eyes turned to Sam and me, who had been together for

several years, and were decidedly not engaged, and never going to be engaged, as far as I was concerned.

"Innnnteresting!" I said jovially, trying to not squash the creative spirit of these two young girls, but also wanting to set the record straight that . . . *not in a million years*. "That's so fun, you guys! I love it. *Lovvvve it*. And even though there will never be a wedding, like, never, ever, ever, I'm certainly not above owning a wedding dress. Especially if it's designed by two glamour-pusses like you." Then I tried my best Tim Gunn impersonation and said, "Make it work, people!" motioning my hand to send them away.

They weren't going anywhere.

"Mama," Hazel implored. "It's going to be covered in butterflies. All. The. Butterflies."

Awwww. Nope.

"Come on," said Sidney, Rosie's bright-eyed little brother. "Just get married already!"

And then all the kids, including our little Hazel, started chanting, "Get! Married! Get! Married! Get! Married!" They began stomping around Sam's parents' house like a marching band in Hanna Andersson pajama sets. "Get! Married! Get! Married! Get! Married!" Hazy was starry-eyed over the grand gesture, vigorously marching along with the cousins, not because she gave a rip if we got married or not but because that girl loves a parade.

It was time for Sam to take the wheel and shut this silliness down. We were with his side of the family, after all. He could be a temporary grump and get away with it. I was a great mother, but I was literally *born* to be a cool aunt—any form of fun-killing would cramp my style.

Sam was not inherently anti-marriage like me, but since I'd taken it off the table on our third or fourth date—it was as plain as, "I never want to get married, so please don't ask"—we hadn't really talked about it much. At some point, I had asked him if it bothered him that, if he stuck with me, he could go his whole life and never become a husband or have a wife. Was that dream-crushing at all for him? He responded that other than wanting to throw an amazing party at the Farm (the Russells were exceptional at doing this), he didn't feel any particular yearning for a legal marriage. There might have been a slight displeasure in his voice as he answered me, but it also could have been because I tended to ask these big life questions when the Celtics were playing, specifically when Jaylen Brown was shooting a three-pointer, so maybe my timing was off.

"Lys doesn't want to get married, guys. Leave her alone!" Sam told the cousin crew.

Rosie, future Madame President, found that response grossly unsatisfactory.

"Alyssa," she said, as if I were on the stand. "What would you say if Sam asked you to marry him right now?"

I looked around the room for some assistance. All I could find were crumbs from my second slice of rhubarb pie. (Pie from Maine, I would marry twice.) Where were the grown-ups to manage this absurd conversation? And then I realized: All the grown-ups wanted to know the answer too! In fact, all the grown-ups were at the edge of their dining room seats, ears perked, wineglasses topped off, waiting to hear what I would say if Sam actually proposed. When I turned to Sam for backup yet again, he, too, appeared to be an inquiring mind. The audacity!

Come on, people, really?

Well, it doesn't happen often, but I was caught off guard. It had been a while since I'd distilled my feelings on marriage. Sometimes I wondered if I conflated my anxiety around having an actual "wedding," having called off not one but *three* of them in the past, with my disdain for the concept of marriage itself. Pretty sure I wasn't so stoked on either, but perhaps it was worth some reexamination.

I knew I loved Sam. There was no question there. It's not so edgy and it's not so fringe, but I was committed to being with him, and *only* him, for the long run. And in living together and having kids together, we certainly experienced many of the same rewards and amenities associated with marriage, rewards and amenities that I would not trade in for the world: a comfy and cozy domestic life, exciting and shared plans for the future, free hugs, good sex whenever you want it, someone who understands and follows all your nuanced work entanglements, someone to pay the sitter when you're out of cash and run to the market when you're craving chips and salsa, someone with whom you can lie on the couch and apropos of nothing turn to and say, *These are the best days of our lives, babe*—and know that they already *know*.

We were not a perfect couple, but we cherished our life together. We were not the lovebirds who finished each other's sentences, but we were the partners who told each other everything. My impulse to throw daggers when I was stressed out made me sometimes hard to live with; his quiet nature made him seem occasionally detached. When I told strangers that I peed when I sneezed—every single time, full pee—Sam shuddered at my existence. When he rummaged through our trash can of dirty diapers and piles of spaghetti *just* to recycle one plastic straw, I wanted him gone for good. When we fought, I went to war. When we relaxed, he wouldn't mind a little weed.

The only real, concrete, ongoing conflict for me was that Sam was not a Jew. This was not just because I wished for a partner who would feel emotional when I lit the Shabbos candles or kissed a mezuzah or joyfully sang "Shalom Alechem" with Hazel and River but because I often lamented that Sam would never fully understand me on account of that striking difference in our upbringing and faith. Our cultural differences were not subtle. They frequently came out in the spiritual, the political, and the mundane. Whenever I watched him respectfully tidy our kids' messes at a restaurant so the waiter wouldn't be burdened by the shit show, I would sneer to myself, "Such a goy." When I'd brawl with my mother, and swear that I'd never speak to her again, only to call her five minutes later with a random thought about wallpapering River's bedroom, Sam often wondered if we had all gone mad. Do I wish he were more *Hamisha*? Yes. Does he wish I ate lobster? Nah, he doesn't care about that.

Ralph Waldo Emerson said, "To be great is to be misunderstood." But then again, isn't being understood—especially by your life partner—the quintessential marker of happiness? Which one was it? Did we have to understand each other completely? Could we live in a world in which "I-love-you-but-I-don't-quite-get-you" was always our starting point? Would that maybe be the thing that kept us challenged by each other? I hoped so.

For the most part, Sam and I were very, very happy and extremely compatible. We took excellent care of each other, running on trust and respect and mutual empowerment, and though it wasn't all slow dancing and bouquets of sunflowers, our relationship was the right relationship for me. Our love language was our children—they were our periscope into each other—which is not to say that we didn't share other passions and desires, but we were deeply bound by Hazel and River, and I would never let anything interfere with that. Especially something as risky as marriage.

"Time's up. What's your answer?" Rosie pressed.

"Okay," I said as chirpily as possible. "If Sam asked me to marry him right now, I would probably say, 'Thank you for asking, my darling, but we are perfect the way we are.'"

"WRONG ANSWER!" screamed all the young ones, and maybe a few of the grown-ups.

Thank goodness for Jeje's timing because just as she announced, "The make-your-own-sundae station is ready! First come, first served!" I was ready to put the subject (and River) to bed. All the kids skadoodled to the kitchen and Wedding Dress Court was adjourned for the day.

On the eight-hour drive home from the Farm that Sunday, I thought long and hard about my beliefs on marriage. Societally, that is, not just for myself personally. I was a "relationship expert" after all. And I had a daughter to raise. A daughter who would eventually wonder if she should become a wife. Shouldn't I have a more defined point of view on the subject, beyond this idea that getting married was just . . . stupid?

Well. It's not just that. I happen to believe that marriage is stupid, and obsolete.

A short tangent. I recently filed a Sex Diary about Scott, a twenty-eight-year-old bisexual therapist. One day, Scott went swimming at the Y. He felt horny afterward. So, on his way back to his apartment, he made a detour to some secret "glory hole" in Park Slope. The hole—which was exactly what it sounds like, a hole—was drilled into a wall inside some unlocked house near Prospect Park. He felt confident it was a safe and healthy situation. Scott walked in, inserted himself into the hole, got sucked off, left, and picked up spicy ramen afterward. Now, it's not necessarily *my* fantasy (barring the ramen), but everything about that scenario kind of makes sense to me.

Marriage, however, does not.

Let me begin by saying I am all for having a Forever Love, but I think the legal contract is insane. Shit happens. People go crazy. Good citizens of the world get caught up in dangerous infatuations and affairs. Or heartbreakingly beautiful, if fucked-up, ones. Mensches get caught jerking off on Zooms. Awesome humans start to hate each other's faces. Things go sideways. Love runs out. I don't mean to sound like a cynic, because I sincerely don't think any of that will happen to me and Sam or most of the great couples I know, but that stuff *does* happen. And when it does, who wants to deal with several endless years of miserable, all-consuming, toe-curling paperwork on top of all the other pain?

Second, I am wholeheartedly opposed to the notion that getting married is an essential milestone for a happy life, and I simply won't endorse it. It's just too punishing for the people who never partner up; it leaves too many good people behind. There is something so backward about this narrative that once you've reached a certain age, if you've gotten married, you've succeeded, and if you're still single, you screwed up. I'm sorry but that's a big fuckin' lie and I'd love to put an end to it. And worse than being a lie, it's just mean to those who chose a nonlinear life path. Thriving in life without a partner—whether it's by choice or not—signifies so much more bravado and character to me. Frankly, I cannot comprehend why our culture doesn't idolize the iconoclastic Singles instead of the Perfect Marrieds. Let's flip the script, already. *Who's with me?*

Lastly, I've heard people say that the best part about being married is that it means you have to stick it out, no matter what happens. That one kind of baffles me. Back to my first point, why would you want to stick together if things got really brutal? Beyond that, shouldn't we have more faith in the foundation of our relationships, with or without a big hunk of wedding cake stored in the freezer? Sam and I are not married, but we could never just . . . bounce. Even if we weren't raising children together, it's not like we'd have a rocky few weeks and just vanish from each other's lives—that couldn't happen even if we wanted it to.

While we're on the topic of those rocky few weeks or months or years, I also think not being married makes fighting much less intense and erosive. Here's how I explain that to my married friends: Let's say things are bad at home. You hate your husband. You're so out of sync. He did something so unforgivable. And it's terrifying because now you're trapped. And you married the wrong man. And what the hell will you do now? Do you need to get divorced? How will you ever undo everything? Anxiety. Regret. Panic. It all just builds and builds. *How could you not completely fall to pieces from that?*

On the other hand, as a Non-Married, a bad fight, or lousy few weeks, goes something like this: "My partner seriously pissed me off. He is the worst. I'm going to leave him tomorrow. But first, BRB, gonna get a prosecco with my friend Pippa. Okay, I'm back. *Hi. Sorry.* Wanna watch *Succession*?!"

There is a very good chance I don't know what I'm talking about here, that I've been unmarried for so long that these are the things I tell myself for coping and self-validation and it's all a little bit *mashugana*. I am willing to accept that, while also staying tough on my no-marriage policy. And to be fair, it should be said that many of my closest friends have enviable marriages with a sense of closeness and togetherness that to me proves that marriage can be an embodiment of love like nothing else.

In our first apartment together in Carroll Gardens, Sam and I lived above Noah and Stephanie Plener, a couple with three incredible little girls and ten thousand tutus, disco balls, unicorn tattoos, magical crystals, and bubble gum toothpastes. Our bedroom was above Noah and Stephanie's bedroom, and night after night, they kept us awake with the loud and wild sound of . . . laughter. Literally, every single night they would put their kids to bed and then laugh each other to sleep like naughty little devils in Parachute sateen sheets. While Sam would often lie in bed reading *The New Yorker* or *American Cinematographer,* I would lie there listening, while smiling, to the fuzzy sounds of Noah saying something hilarious and Stephanie cracking up. By comparison, our dynamic was so much less . . . dynamic. Comparison is the thief of joy, I know. And yet, what a great marriage.

Here's another marriage tale that sat just right with me: My friends Marjolein and Joost are a lovely, leggy Dutch couple living in Brooklyn. They have three blond children who should all be child models, and the kids and I adore them. I recently saw Marj and her daughter at Brooklyn Bridge Park.

"Where's Joost?" I asked, noticing he wasn't around only after an entire dissertation on why kids can't live without their effing water bottles. Hazel and I watch a lot of *Naked and Afraid*—we both know no one dehydrates after eight minutes.

"I don't know. . . . He's been gone for three days," Marj said casually.

"What? Like, he's missing?" I asked, a little too thirsty for the lowdown.

"No, no. He's not missing. He just wanted to be alone for a few days and I didn't ask for details. He needed some 'me time.' Why would I tell him no? He'll be back soon."

That's all. He communicated a need, she listened *and* heard him, and it was literally as simple as that. Joost was let loose. No questions asked. No resentment. No backlash. No residual anger. No guilt. No drama. And I thought that was very healthy and admirable.

The next time I saw Marj, she was headed off to Costa Rica. Alone! "Quid pro quo," she whispered to me, with a wink. I love Europeans. Well, *most* Europeans.

Anyway. If I can profess anything about love and marriage with certainty, it is this: There are intimate little love stories to be embraced everywhere, and the best ones usually have nothing to do with off-the-shoulder Carolina Herrera or on-the-bone lamb chops, though both sound divine. There are intimate little love stories with friends, strangers, lovers, celebrity crushes, fertility doctors, and anonymous sperm donors—and those unconventional and certainly unexplainable relationships can be breathtakingly rich. My mother is in an intimate relationship with every single MTA bus driver in Brooklyn. My father was in an intimate relationship with Valerie, a teller from Dime Savings Bank, who sometimes seemed like the only person in the world who listened to him, and who recently died (he's sad she won't read this). My sister was in an intimate relationship with Sonny the Breakfast Sandwich Man, who had a street cart seven floors below her living room window, and who always knew when she needed a loving wave. (I asked Sonny to do a Sex Diary and things got weird, but that's a different story.) There's an intimate love story in the airstream as you read this on the subway or an airplane or a beach. There are love stories that live in heaven. Over life-changing cappuccinos. Over motorcycles ridden by mystery men. And there are love stories that begin with a Bloody Mary with extra olives and a vintage Johnny Cash T-shirt—and end, hopefully, never. These are life's most precious jewels. I have an overflowing vault of them.

And that, my friends, is what gives me . . . all the butterflies.

twenty-seven

The Final Breakup

*D*o *you know where I can get, like, two therapy sessions?* I texted my psychologist friend and neighbor, Sara, from the bathtub. After I hit send, I put the phone down on my Urban Outfitters bath mat that read *Hello lovely,* and tried to soak my body and relax my mind a little.

A few seconds later, Sara rang. With my hand trickling with soapy water, I reached out of the tub, pressed speaker, and said, "Hey, mama."

"So, as a professional, I can't really advise you to see a therapist only twice," she said, in good humor. "But as a friend, tell me what's going on, and maybe we can come up with a plan."

"First of all, I'm naked," I announced.

"Great, welcome to psychotherapy," she responded.

"So, everything is fine. We're fine. No drama. But . . . we're finalizing Hazel's adoption papers soon, and changing her last name from Shelasky to Russell, and I've never had any anxiety about any of this, and yet, here I am, kind of, sort of freaking out—and lashing out, and I'm not sure why. So I think I need, like, two hours of emotional unpacking just to move through it in the healthiest possible way."

Sara and I agreed to take a nice, long walk sometime in the next few days and *try* not to flake on each other. We were both working mothers, we were still living in the pandemic, school wasn't fully reopened yet, so life was a real grind. That said, our walk-and-talk would be just as girlfriends. For real therapy, she sent me some recommendations and gently suggested I use the term "looking for short-term help" rather than admit I only had time for about 120 minutes of analysis.

"Not a minute more," I reminded her.

As far as changing Hazel's last name from Shelasky to Russell, that was primarily a practical matter. School forms, bills, taxes, and especially travel were bound to get complicated if we all had different last names. I mean, I once got arrested at a Chilean airport for trying to enter the country with a Pink Lady apple in my pocketbook. Who knows what could happen if Samuel Z. Russell tried to take Hazel Delilah Shelasky out of the country on a special vacation. I didn't want to find out. I also never wanted people to question whether or not my kids, who at this point had different last names, were "full siblings." Because, of course they were "full siblings"! That was a sensitive issue to me. Hazel and River were brother and sister, and if you wanted to get into semantics, you better beware. To take it even further, I especially never wanted anyone questioning if Sam was Hazel's "real dad," either. Nothing about our family's history was hushed, but why not streamline the last names to preemptively avoid any unnecessary remarks if Hazel didn't want them? Had I not been an established writer, I probably would have changed my last name to Russell too. But for now, I was content with three Russells and one Shelasky. After all, a little Shelasky goes a long way.

Hazel knows the truth, or whatever truths a five-year-old brain can handle, about her story. She knows that I made her from a little seed that a doctor planted inside my body. She knows that there's another word for that seed, and that word is "sperm." But "it's kind of a silly word," as she says. Someday, in the future, we will talk more about that seed and where it came from, and who it came from. But only a private whisper inside will tell me when the time is right for that.

Hazel also knows that when she was born, there was no daddy, only *my* daddy, Baba, and he was the first person to hold her. She knows that for a few months on earth, it was just Hazy and Mommy, and that those were some of the most glorious memories of my life. Hazel is well versed in the story of when I met Sam. . . . Well, she tells the story like this: "Mommy met a boy named Sammy, and he begged and begged to be part of our family, and finally we said, 'Okaaaay! Fine! Sure! Sure, you can be in our family!' And that's when Hazy got a dada. And I love my dada!!!" And then she usually jumps into Sam's arms and asks if he wants to watch *The Sound of Music* or *Annie* together. (When Daddy Warbucks gives Annie that locket, we all completely lose it.)

So, Hazel Delilah Shelasky would become Hazel Shelasky Russell. (RIP Delilah; I think you're a fabulous name.) When we carefully and thoughtfully sat Hazel down over a big plate of chocolate chip pancakes to tell her about the "exciting" and "maybe confusing" name change, she plainly told us that she already thought Russell *was* her last name, and then she threw her arms in the air and hollered, "More whipped cream, please!" So that was that.

The legal adoption would be a lot more involved, for all of us. We needed to fill out so many forms that Sam had to buy a new printer just to make a dent in them. Then we needed to collect a bunch of personal information, have our loved ones write letters, get several statements notarized, and schedule a home visit from a New York State social worker. It was an epic time commitment, especially when I needed all my spare seconds to go to my work life. But, as I continued to tell myself, if we couldn't make this our most important priority, then we probably shouldn't be doing it in the first place.

Per my call to Sara, I did notice some inner tension as I helped Sam get everything in order, though—and I wasn't sure where it was coming from. The only way to describe the feeling was as one of mixed emotions. Sam had been my partner and Hazel's father since she was seven months old. She has no memories of life without him. So it was as if nothing was going to change, and yet, everything was going to change. On one hand, there was the unspeakable beauty of providing my child with a second loving parent, and on the other hand, I was relinquishing the profound honor of being the only person she ever belonged to. It felt like both an extraordinary gain, and an extraordinary loss.

But we were a family, and I didn't want it any other way, so what was that sense of loss *really* about?

Hazel was living, breathing, dancing proof of the resplendent powers of living life differently. But within Hazel's sheer existence also lived so much of my romantic history. To tell our story, which I have always done with such pride and candor, was to preserve all my heartbreak, mistakes, rejections, and disappointments. As a result of writing about my road to motherhood, and being so open about our journey, those memories were so muscular and those heartaches were still so evocative, and I wasn't sure that was serving me so well anymore.

My ex-boyfriends, my bad breakups, they were not all romantic misadventures. They were love traumas. And I've used those love traumas to move through the world. They've played a tremendous role in my career. And they dominate my road-to-happiness story— but lately, it felt like my old flames and all the pain that came with them were trespassing. I didn't want the memories around anymore. I didn't want them around as I raised my kids. And I didn't want them around as Sam and I embraced our future. Now was the time to stop outrunning my heartbreaks. They needed to be erased from my hard drive for good. All this is to say, I had one last breakup left in me: it was time to break up with the breakups of my past. But I had no idea how to do that.

"You have any time to go to the notary public together later today?" Sam asked one morning, stopping me in my tracks as I packed Hazel's PB and J for her half day of "Pod," while responding to a *Sex Diaries* docuseries email, and chugging coffee, *and* randomly wondering if River, with his fine, gentile blond locks, would ever get lice.

"Um. No. Sweetie, I don't even have time to—"

When I looked up from the cutting board, an enraptured Hazel was swinging upside down from Sam's arms and a beaming River was on Sam's back, and I was acutely aware that life did not get better than this.

"Never mind," I said, taking in the adorableness and drawing in a long deep breath. "Let's do it. I'll move some things around."

I texted a potential sex diarist that we'd have to reschedule our Zoom session. She wanted to write about going down on a woman for the first time, but had reservations about her southern Christian family reading the piece and identifying her. My job always entailed something urgent and delicate and scandalous, but this would have to wait until later.

Just before noon, Sam and I were at a FedEx Office on the charming and unremarkable Montague Street in Brooklyn Heights to get the adoption paperwork notarized. The shop was open, but empty inside. "Hello? Anyone here?" I called out loudly. Underwhelmed by the food options on the street, I was hungry and cranky. Plus, I wanted to deal with that *Sex Diaries* stuff and not wait for some stranger to finish his Chipotle Lifestyle Bowl in the back office.

"He's on his lunch break," I reported back to Sam. "Maybe we should come back another time." But Sam wasn't paying attention. He was shuffling through the paperwork in his folders, flipping through page after page, making sure there were no loose ends, and organizing everything into tidy little stacks. I had never seen him look so businesslike or disciplined.

"Okey dokey, we'll stay." I shrugged to no one in particular.

After another ten minutes, the notary public walked out front and stood apathetically behind the counter, eye to eye with us. He did not say so much as one word. He was in fact, more or less, the opposite of a Lifestyle Bowl.

"Hi!" I said. "Good lunch? Chipotle hits the spot once in a while but . . . Montague Street has so much wasted potential, don't you think? The Vietnamese coffee at Hanco's is actually quite good. Have you ever tried that?"

No response. The notary public had no personality. An "NP!" as my mother would call people with *no personalities* or those we just couldn't crack (and there weren't many). It was actually kind of perfect that our NP was the ultimate NP.

Sam laid the paperwork on the counter, with various colored tabs indicating where and what needed to be stamped and signed, by all of us, and we looked at him for what to do next. The NP stated that he had to oversee (with his dead eyes) us do our signatures first.

"You need a pen, Sammy?" I sang, turning to him. That's when I saw that Sam was in an odd state, nervously fishing around in his pockets for a pen, then ruffling through his backpack for one. It was taking him so long to find something so simple, that instead I reached over the counter and snagged a ballpoint pen lodged under the credit card machine. Either the NP didn't notice or didn't care.

"Here!" I said, placing the pen in his hands.

The first few pages required Sam's signature only, not mine, so as I waited for him to do his part, I impatiently checked the time on my iPhone, thinking, *Let's get this show on the road already*. I had to get back to work. Plus, on top of "Sex Diaries," I had my first therapy call later in the day, which Sam did not know about, and I needed to budget extra time for that. None of this was going into the mail until after said therapy session either (which Sam also did not know about). I was not in the business of keeping secrets from my partner, but these days we never had time to talk about anything other than childcare, work schedules, or occasionally President Biden or *Ted Lasso*. At some point, I'd tell him everything, once I knew what *everything* was really about. Right now we just had to sign and go.

But then I looked closely at Sam, who was hunched over the paperwork, presenting not like the hot, cool dad with a gentle soul and a ski slope nose that I always saw him as but like a jittery middle-aged man who was going through something. I wasn't sure what was happening, but as I took in his energy, I realized that he was so moved by the happiness and realness of making this official, that he was overwhelmed. He was so overwhelmed that when he flipped to the first page that required his signature, I noticed that his hands were shaking. He had dreamed of this moment for so long. He looked up at me, smiling, and his pale blue eyes were twinkling with tears. I moved a few inches in his direction, put my arm around his waist, and whispered, "I'll sign first, okay?"

As I brought the pen to the page and scribbled *Alyssa Shelasky* across each and every dotted line, I looked up at the NP and said, "This amazing man right here? He is legally adopting my daughter.

Thank you for being part of this, sir." I got nothing. Bubkes. But at least I made things awkward enough that Sam could not help but laugh and blush a little. Then I swung my right hip into his and said, "It's all you, my dear." He took the pen and finished up the rest.

We walked out of that office hand in hand, with the adoption paperwork safe in my leather tote bag, prepared to be sent whenever I felt ready. And in the middle of Montague Street—which I still believed needed a major makeover—I held him and I kissed him. And in my arms, I felt him relax.

Later that night I went back to my bathtub, fully dressed this time, as I was not hopping in for a soak with Dr Teal's but a virtual therapy session with a woman named Roberta. Like most pandemic moms, the bath was the only place I could sit in my apartment with some privacy.

The session began.

"Look, I'm a very self-aware woman," I said to Roberta, who looked exactly like her name should be Roberta. "I've written about my love life for my entire career, so I've already done a lot of 'the work.' But I was hoping you could help me . . ."

It was tougher than you'd think to say the next line.

"*Let go* . . . of some of it."

"You bet I can," Roberta smirked, with a terrific husky voice and a thick New York accent. "But let me ask you something, Alyssa. How much time do we have?"

In the background of my apartment, I could hear Sam and our kids, the Shelasky-Russell kids, laughing at the dinner table. Fleetwood Mac was playing on Sam's record player. He makes the best quesadillas. I loved our life so much.

I thought about Roberta Klein's question for another second or two, because I like to stay true to my word, and then firmly stated, "As much time as we need."

twenty-eight

A Celebration

You are cordially invited to a celebration on Verona Island...

I was lying on my bed designing an invitation via some chic paper goods website, which was perhaps the daintiest thing I had ever done in my life. Sam was traveling for work.

Hazel, now five *and a half,* was in her room flipping through the Mini Boden catalog and circling outfits that fell under her aesthetic, which could best be described as: eighties aerobics instructor meets Paris Fashion Week—lots of bodysuits, shoulder pads, ripped black lace, studded belts, neon fake nails, and metallic pumps. All she knew, at this point, was that we were hosting a summer soiree, and she had a weekend wardrobe to curate.

River, sixteen months old, was on his step stool, looking out my bedroom window, cheering, per usual, "Twuuuuuuck! Cah! Twaaactah!" Every time an automobile went by, his mind was blown;

it was like he'd *seen the light*! He was also a total bruiser, who, by the end of every day, looked like he'd been in a boxing match gone terribly wrong, or an episode of *Ray Donovan*. He could barely say "banana" and yet I could almost hear him explaining, "But, Ma, you should see the other guy."

My "wedding dress" was still in the works. The cousins in Boston were making the thing whether I liked it or not. They had a virtual mood board and needed my measurements, and of course, Hazel's final approval on everything. My sister's kids were also looped in on the project, thanks to Hazel's enthusiasm. My nephew Charlie created a spreadsheet of the final accessories that needed to be sourced, along with a budget. (Wharton, are you reading this? Please confirm to Laurie "Dodo" Temkin Shelasky that you are reading this.) And my niece Phoebe had begun jewelry designing with one billion little beads that, ideally, River would not choke on.

But I was not wearing the gown to a wedding. I had something else in mind, hence the party invitations.

Earlier in the week, I had sent out a group text with the following words: *Who wants to join us for a special night at the Farm this August? Send me all your open weekends.*

I smirked to myself, knowing they would all start to speculate.

Like clockwork, my mother was the first to respond: "Tick season?" she asked, with a bug emoji.

A second later Sam's mother texted back: "Blueberry season!" with a shooting star emoji.

Such is the beauty of the Shelasky-Russell blend.

Hazel's legal adoption would be finalized by August, and I wanted to throw a big bash in honor of our happy news. This would be our most special night with our most special people. A collective, creative, heart-bursting gathering to honor our union as a family, with *our* families, and with champagne, and a decadent cake that need not be white fondant. That's everything I told Hazel, at least, as we got ready for bed that night. Oh, I also guaranteed a cotton candy machine, because what is life without some harmless rebellion?

When Sam is away, Hazel likes to sleep in my bed. It's one of our favorite rituals. This night was no different. The teeth were brushed. The books were read. The lights were down. It was time to say good night. HBO had officially green-lit the *Sex Diaries* docuseries and I was filming early in the morning.

"Ah! Just us!" Hazel said, curling up into my arms, under the covers, in her long, worn-in nightgown. "Just like when I was a baby. Right, Mama?"

"Right, Hazy." I pulled her in closer. She smelled like Warm Vanilla Sugar mist from Bath & Body Works and I took full responsibility for that.

Sometimes late at night, Hazel asks me the most amazing questions. Kids are such little philosophers and theologians. It's kind of astounding. Some of her questions have included: Is there a TV in heaven? Does hair have feelings? Where do fairies sleep? Are there sidewalks on the moon? When will the earth be safe? How do flowers know how to dance? Can Hashem hear us laugh? When you die, how long will it be until I see you again? She is my muse.

On this night, her question wasn't particularly existential, but her mind was wandering.

"Can I make a speech at the party in Maine?"

"Of course! You can say or do anything. It's our night. We're celebrating our family! That's a terrific idea."

She grinned, and cuddled closer, her skinny body like a heat lamp in a ponytail scrunchie.

"But what if I don't know what to say?" she asked, not quite as sleepy as I wanted her to be. "Can we do it together?"

"Definitely. We'll say something together. Now go to bed, my love."

A few seconds passed.

"Mommy, what should we say together?"

We were both tired. But I wanted to send her into dreamland with something loving and comforting. It took a moment for the words to find me, but suddenly, after all those years, after all this life, they streamed right into my consciousness. Finally I remembered the meditation from Switzerland.

"How about we do this, Hazy? I'll say a line, and you repeat it after me."

"Like I'm your echo," she said in the sweetest voice I'd ever heard.

"Exactly," I said, kissing her cheek. "Like you're my echo. Okay, here we go . . ."

May you be happy.

May you be happy.

May you be healthy.

May you be healthy.

May you be safe.

May you be safe.

May you live with ease.

May you live with ease.

. . .

The party in Maine had one more secret meaning to me.

Nearly twenty years had passed since I ran away from normal at Chelsea Piers. I knew I'd land on my feet, but I had no idea just how many times I'd get knocked down first. I knew I wanted to live a cool little life, but I don't think I realized that the cost of living a cool little life was . . . the wild and relentless ride of *life itself*.

Because, since that afternoon on the West Side Highway, I've put my heart on the line more times than I can count. I've moved in and out of seventeen different apartments within four chaotic cities. There were too many sexy and terrible boyfriends, all of whom either lifted me up like a narcotic drug or dragged me down like an undertow. Several heartbreaks (almost) broke me. I learned how to *not* have a baby, how to have a baby *without* a man, and how to make a baby with a country boy. I also had two chemical pregnancies and a miscarriage. My ambition, and my agent, took me on seventy impossible television pitches, usually while massively pregnant and on the brink of a stroke. I learned how to write a memoir, how to fry a zucchini blossom, and how to talk about anilingus on camera with class. I lost truly exceptional friends to drugs, suicide, terrorism, and terminal illness. I made mom friends, work friends, and lifelong best friends who were right by my side for all of the above, even when they had their own tough stuff unfolding. I watched my parents grow older, and experience the profound happiness of life as Dodo and Baba, and I witnessed my little sister become a stellar mother and a woman of the world.

So what I'm trying to say is this: It took me almost two long decades—from my young adulthood all the way to my midlife—to discover what I had been running toward that day at Chelsea Piers. Nothing came easy. There were years and years of feeling around in the dark. I picked up every seashell and listened for the ocean, stumbled through every forest, foraging for objects that shimmered and that I could call my own. And finally the search was over. I had the answer. It was them. It was them all along. My daughter. My son. My partner. I was running toward *them*. They were my destiny. They were my blessings. They were my transcendence. And now I was ready to celebrate.

Acknowledgments

This Might Be Too Personal is dedicated to my dear friend Alison Greenspan, who fought for my success as a writer until her very last days fighting cancer. Alison, I will remember you with profound gratitude for the rest of my life. I would do anything to walk into a room together again.

Thank you to my mother, the legendary Laurie Temkin Shelasky, who has loved and supported me like no other. Mom, you have helped make all my dreams come true. Without you, I would have nothing. And to my father, Edward Shelasky, thank you for the 24-7 encouragement and closeness, and mostly for being our hero on the night I had Hazy. It should go on the record that my parents also watched my children, did my laundry, and unloaded my dishwasher almost every single day while I struggled (understatement!) to make this book deadline. They are the best parents and grandparents in the world.

To my sister, Rachel, you astound me with your beauty, goodness, and grace. Thank you for being you, and bonus thank-you for all the marketing and branding you handled for me. I love you MTLI and I will stand by you forever.

To all my nieces and nephews, especially Charles and Phoebe Karasik, thank you for being your sweet and precious selves. It is my greatest pleasure watching you all grow up, but also, *please stop growing up*.

To the extraordinarily loving and giving Temkins, and everyone in the immediate and extended Shelasky, Karasik, Russell, Jewett, Marcus, Goldsworthy, and Gordon families, thank you dearly for your warm, beautiful, and open hearts. Ron and Jeanne Russell, I absolutely cherish you.

I'd like to take a moment to honor my wonderful cousin Emily Wright, who tragically passed away as these pages went into publication. Em, if only this was a book about *your* stories instead of mine, we'd be sailing off into the sunset on a mega-yacht together. I adored you, Emmy, and you are deeply missed by all of us.

Love and gratitude to my best friends forever: Shelley Reinstein, Danyelle Freeman, Beth Daigle, Pippa Lord, Raquel Balsam, and Stephanie Plener. And to the good women who helped me with this book: Shelley's unstoppable team at Autumn, Lisette Sand-Freedman and her extraordinary Shadows, Danielle Praport at Zaria PR, Ilana Alperstein at Mona Creative, Carolyn Murnick, Alexis Adlouni, Tina Malhotra, Sarah Treem, Cat Marnell, and the great Vanessa Grigoriadis.

To my treasured Longmeadow crew: Anzo, Kates, Courtney, and our Jean, I love you guys. To your families: the Cothrans, Egans, Fosters, and Rogers, you are still my favorite people on earth. And to Margaret (Margie) Smith Agnoli, Smitty's mom, who graciously helped me with his chapter, thank you for sharing your remarkable spirit and strength.

Thank you to my amazing family at The Landing (you know who you are!), who fed my kids chicken nuggets around-the-clock and nourished me with cappuccinos and/or Pinot Noir when I was too exasperated for Adulting. We never would have survived the last few years without you. You saved us!

To our chosen family, Veronica "V" Phillip, Sam and I can never thank you enough for taking care of our children and infusing such brilliance and integrity into our lives. You have a place in our hearts (and here at 14I) always.

Ross Flournoy, you are a rare and gorgeous gift. Jill and Tom Flournoy, thank you for creating that rare and gorgeous gift. And while we're in the magical human being department, thank you to Josh Resnick, Gina Resnick, Eric Cook, Doug Robinson, Pavia Rosati, and Rosemary Maggiore just for being you.

For a long time, I described my literary agent, Meg Thompson of Thompson Literary Agency, as "an even hotter Megan Fox," and that was very wrong of me, because she is soooo much more than that! Meg, you made this book happen in the middle of a pandemic while we were both stuck (I mean, responsibly social distancing) in Maine, and you made it look easy. You are such a good woman and such a fierce agent. And because of you, there is Hannah Phillips at St. Martin's Press, who generously ended all our five hundred–plus emails with, *Have I told you lately how much I love this book?* Well, Hannah, have I told you lately how much I love you??? You are wise and kind and the world is a better place because you are in it. Thank you for everything!

Speaking of my team (LOL), thank you to my ever-loyal and hardworking agents, Zach Carlisle and Ari Lever, at ICM. Thank you to my excellent lawyer, Todd Rubenstein, at Morris Yorn. And thank you to my accountant, and pal, Alan Goldberger.

To everyone at "The Cut"—especially Jordan Larson—I am so honored to work with you. And to the original *Sex Diaries* docuseries dream team—Jenny Carchman, Allyson Luchak, and Alexandra Nikolchev—you're brilliant and thoughtful beyond words. To everyone at Vox and HBO, a genuine thank-you for inviting me to the party and letting me stay late.

Sam Russell. I can't bear to think about my life had you not walked in that door many moons ago. You know I worship Patti Smith, and this quote from her says it all: "When we awoke he greeted me with his crooked smile, and I knew he was my knight." I love you, Sammy. You are my knight. To our pride and joy, Mister River: you sweet, funny, ridiculously handsome boy—I love you more than words! And to Hazel, the heart and soul of this book, thank you for being my Hazy. I love you, Zuzu, Ha-Ha, Honeybear. May you always look out into the world, as you do every night, and dream of the extraordinary beauty that awaits.